The Older I Get, The Smarter My Mother Was

May you always be blessed with laughter—
Sally

Sara Jane Coffman

ISBN: 9781793310729
Imprint: Independently published

With Special Thanks to

My good friend Diane, who edits my work and keeps me humble by oftentimes telling me she can't talk to me until after she feeds her dog.

Also by Sara Jane Coffman

The Misadventures of a Single Woman

There's No Such Thing as a Comfortable Bra

I'm Tired, I'm Hungry, and My Feet Are Always Cold

Other Titles Considered for This Book

There were several titles in the running for the title of this book. It was my hairdresser who came up with "The Older I Get, The Smarter My Mother Was" one day while she was trying to even out the hair on the left side of my head with the hair on the right (which I'd been trimming at home myself).

We were swapping stories about our mothers, and both admitted we didn't always appreciate our mothers' words of wisdom when we were growing up. But we wished our mothers were still here so we could tell them how much they influenced us.

Another title that was in the running was: "Just Shoot Me" -- the battle cry of all women who are overwhelmed. (Are there women who *aren't* overwhelmed?) It's my friend Rhonda's favorite saying. I'll call Rhonda on a Monday morning and ask her how her weekend went. (She runs her own business, and has a husband, two daughters, two sons-in-law, a precocious, red-headed, two-year old grandson, four dogs who don't get along with each other, and two cats, who, of course, don't get along with the dogs.)

Her answer to my question, more often than not, is: "Just shoot me."

The third title I considered was: "It's 6:00 p.m. and We're Still in Chicago." That title came, not from the old question: "It's late, do you know where your children are?", but from a bus trip I recently took to tour the ethnic neighborhoods of Chicago.

Now, if you make all the green lights, it's a good two-hour trip from Lafayette, Indiana to Chicago, Illinois. I almost cancelled the trip because I was going to have a busy day the following day and it was important for me to get to bed early. But I went ahead and went, believing their promise that we'd be back in Lafayette by dinnertime. We weren't.

After we finished our last museum, we got on the bus and headed back home. I'd lost track of where we were, but when I looked out the window, I saw that we were *north* of Chicago. We had to traverse Chicago from one end to the other – IN RUSH HOUR. Then the tour guide announced we'd be stopping FOR AN HOUR on the way home so people could have dinner. I looked at my watch, took out a notepad, and penned: It's 6:00 and we're still in Chicago.

Everybody's had that experience. When you realize that where you are is not where you wanted – or planned -- to be.

The fourth title in the running was: "It Seemed Like a Good Idea at the Time." You can probably identify with that one as well. When we were young and dumb – or at least, younger and dumber – we made choices that *did* seem like a good idea at the time.

A fifth possible title was: "Say what?" How many times do people say things to you that don't make sense, and you just want to look at them and say: "Say WHAT?"

There were some food titles I also considered. "I Paid For it, So I Have to Eat it." And "I Want to Eat the Kitchen" which is every woman's lament when they're under stress or get the midnight munches.

Well, enough with the titles. On with the stories. May they tickle your funny bones and make you LOL (Laugh Out Loud) . . .

Table of Contents

I Have the Best Friends

I'm blessed with having a number of really close friends who are all crazy about me. But they're careful not to show it.

Although we exchange emails, I much prefer talking to them on the phone. A typical phone call finds us catching up with each other on what's been going on in our lives. But oftentimes, I'll call when I need an immediate answer to a question.

For instance, sometimes when I'm making dinner, I'll find I'm missing a key ingredient, so I'll call Diane. "The recipe calls for apple juice! I don't have any! What can I use instead?"

I also call when I need help with my writing. "I'm stuck! Here's what I've written so far. How should I end it?"

I also call when I've put my foot in my mouth. My friends are much more savvy at interpersonal relationships than I am, and I rely on them to help me get myself out of the messes I get into. "Here's what I did." (They groan.) "Now what should I do?"

Most of the time when I'm in the middle of an emergency, my friends will stop what they're doing so we can talk. But they each have their priorities. Take Diane.

Diane will always drop what she's doing to take my calls. Except if I call when she's feeding her dog.

Diane has a rescue dachshund named Angel who has digestive issues, so, three times a day, she feeds him by hand (so he doesn't eat too fast). If I happen to call when she's in the middle of feeding Angel --or getting ready to feed Angel -- she tells me she'll call me back.

She always does. But I know where I stand when it comes to her dog.

The other time I know not to call her is on Tuesday nights from 8:00 to 9:00 p.m. That's when she watches NCIS. I could be arrested and want her to be my one call from jail, but if it's on a Tuesday night, I know to wait until NCIS is over.

My friend Rhonda and I like to meet for coffee. And she's always ready to do that, except if she has a nail appointment, hair appointment, trip to the vet, or if it's the day when her housekeeper comes to clean her house.

I'm important to her, but not as important as her housekeeper.

This week when I called to make plans, I made sure it wasn't the week she was going to have her house cleaned. But she still was having an especially busy week. She said the only time she could see me was if I rode along with her in the car when she went to volunteer at her daughter's school, take her husband to the wound clinic for his foot, or take one of the dogs to the vet for a CT scan.

Rod is another friend I enjoy being with. Sometimes he goes with me to read jokes when I read stories from my books to various groups around town. He has a wonderful sense of humor, he's a marvelous reader, and audiences love him. But I know not to ask him for his help on a night when there's a Purdue basketball game.

My sister will take my phone calls unless it's on a Sunday afternoon. That's when she takes a nap.

Don takes my calls if he has his hearing aids in and hears the phone.

Last week Lyn told me she'd like to accept my invitation to lunch, but she was getting ready for a garage sale.

My friend Kevin and I have lunch together every Friday. Except for the last Friday of the month because that's when he has his monthly hair appointment. I've suggested that he move his hair appointment to another day, but he says he's been getting his hair cut by the same stylist for forty years at that same time on that same day. And she still only charges him what she charged him forty years ago: $13.00.

I know not to stand between Kevin and his hair cuts.

Occasionally, Fridays don't work for *me* and I suggest moving our lunch date to another day of the week. Sometimes that works; sometimes it doesn't, as you can see from our latest round of emails:

Kevin,

The only day I can have lunch next week is Friday, but I know it's the last Friday of the month, and that's your hair cut day. Here are my ideas:

PLAN A: Cancel your hair appointment and just be shaggy for the next month.

PLAN B: Send me some money so I can go have a nice lunch on my own.

PLAN C: Meet me Friday for *dinner* instead of for lunch.

Sally

Sally,

Very clever! Unfortunately, plans A thru C don't work for me. I'm having more dental work done today, so eating will be iffy. Looks like a week from Friday?

Kevin

Kevin,

Next Friday is O.K. with me. But I had to INFER your devastation about not meeting with me *this* week. I thought I had explained how I expected you to be devastated if we can't meet.

Sally

Sally,

Dang . . . Dang . . . Dang . . . Woe is me . . . Woe is me . . . Woe is me . . . Whatever shall I do now . . . my entire week is RUINED!

Is that better?

Sadly,

Kevin

Kevin,

Much better. I especially enjoyed your selection of the word "sadly." Nice touch.

Sally

Here's our email exchange confirming lunch the following Friday. As you can see, he was trying to adjust our time together as opposed to adjusting the time he spends on his job:

Kevin,

Are we on for lunch? Can we meet at our regular restaurant? And can you come around 11:45 instead of noon? I need to be somewhere at 1:00.

Sally

Hi Sally,

I have a meeting from 11:30 – noon, so I won't be able to get there until 12:15 or so. But a little is better than nothing. (smiley face)

Kevin

Kevin,

O.K. But that means I get to do all the talking.

Sally

Sally,

O.K. But bring a bobble-head with you so my neck won't get sore. . .

Kevin

As you can see, I'm a relatively easy person to get along with, and try to always be accessible to my friends.

Well, except if I'm watching *Say Yes to the Dress*.

Everybody knows I don't answer the phone or respond to emails if I'm watching *Say Yes to the Dress*.

If It Wasn't for *The Twilight Zone*, I Wouldn't Have Survived Kindergarten Camp

When I was growing up, I didn't watch the TV series called *The Twilight Zone*. It wasn't something my family would have been into. But recently, someone recommended the show to me, and I started watching the reruns. They were fascinating! They were clever, well- written, and thought-provoking.

The characters in the shows always found themselves in strange and bizarre situations. When I watched, I tried to put myself in their shoes. How would *I* react to a strange and bizarre situation? Would I freak out, like some of them did? Or would I be able to adapt?

Which brings me to kindergarten camp. Every summer, my friend Pam volunteers in a program at the local elementary school. Underprivileged kids are bussed in, given breakfast, and provided with backpacks filled with school supplies. The program is designed to prepare them for kindergarten in the fall.

Pam saw me at church and encouraged me to volunteer, too. "You'll love it!"

I wasn't so sure, but I agreed to give it a try.

When I arrived the first morning, the kids were still in the cafeteria getting their breakfast. I surveyed the room. The tables were only about a foot off the floor. Kindergarteners must be tiny little people, I thought, to be little enough to sit at tables that low.

The chairs were miniature, too. Fine for the kids. But where was *I* going to sit?

As it turned out, I didn't have to worry about that because I wasn't going to be doing much sitting. In came 25 five-year-olds with their breakfasts. I spent the next fifteen minutes opening milk cartons and juice cartons. Milk cartons are glued shut and impossible to open. And when you stick the straw into a juice carton, the juice squirts out all over the table.

I also opened small bags of cereal and boxes of raisins. And when I wasn't opening things, I was running to the kitchenette to get towels to clean up the spilled milk, juice, cereal, and sticky raisins.

One little boy told me he had to go to the bathroom. No problem. There was a bathroom right inside the classroom. I walked him over, opened the door for him, and waited to make sure he was O.K. When he came out, I asked him if he'd washed his hands.

He looked at me like I was from *The Twilight Zone*.

Back into the bathroom to show him the sink where he could wash his hands.

He came out with wet hands.

"Did you *dry* your hands?"

"There's no towel."

So, we went back in and I showed him the towel dispenser. "See this? You turn this little handle to release the paper towel. Then you tear it off."

He dried his hands.

I did that for about three more little kids, but suddenly there were six more waiting to use the bathroom. So, I decided to make it a group lesson. I took them in as a group and repeated my demonstration. "You turn the little handle on the side, and then rip the paper towel across from one side to the other."

While I was doing this, one little girl pulled down her pants and started using the toilet. *Twilight Zone.*

After breakfast, the teacher gave each student a plastic box filled with pencils, crayons, scissors, and a glue stick. We would be using these things in the future.

After that, she handed out little containers of play dough. One little boy immediately got the scissors out of his box and started cutting the play dough.

"No," Mrs. Ross said gently. "We don't use the scissors to cut the play dough."

Whereupon, the other twenty-four students, ignoring the key word "don't," got their scissors out of their boxes and began cutting their play dough.

After that, she handed out worksheets to color. Twenty-four of the students began to color. The twenty-fifth little boy got his glue stick out and started gluing his sheet of paper to the table.

"No," Mrs. Ross said gently. "We're not going to use the glue stick today."

Whereupon, the other twenty-four students, ignoring the key word "not," got their glue sticks out and began gluing their worksheets.

We managed to pry the glue sticks away and steer everyone back to their crayons. We only found about twenty of the lids to the glue sticks. The other five had disappeared into the *Twilight Zone*.

Now the kids' fingers were sticky with glue. Their fingers stuck to the crayons, to the table, and to the worksheets. Several of them felt a need to touch *me* to show *me* how sticky their fingers were.

Following the crayon activity, it was time for everyone to gather on the mat and listen to Mrs. Ross read a book. She told them to sit "crisscross-applesauce" on the floor with their hands in their laps. She began to read.

I lowered myself into one of the miniature chairs. And surveyed the room. There were twenty-five kids doing twenty-five different things.

One was vigorously, and with great intent, picking his nose.

One was stretched out, relaxing, ostensibly from her ordeal with the scissors and the glue stick.

One was leaning up against the wall, snoring.

Two little girls were facing each other, playing some sort of game with their hands.

One, returning from the bathroom, was trying in vain to pull his zipper up.

One was scratching inside the front of his pants.

One little girl was pulling the sparkles off the tee-shirt of the little girl in front of her.

One was talking on an imaginary cell phone.

One was braiding her hair.

One was sneezing, with the intent, I think, of infecting as many of his classmates as possible.

One was quietly singing the alphabet song.

One had brought his glue stick with him and was applying it to the inside of another little boy's ear.

One was paying attention.

And one was running around the room, with his arms extended, making airplane sounds. Actually, I thought that was a perfectly rational response to having his parents put him on a bus and send him off to kindergarten camp.

Several thoughts ran through my head. First, I hoped that when reading time was over, I'd be able to stand back up.

Second, tomorrow I should probably wear older clothes.

And third, tonight – to prepare for tomorrow -- I should probably watch a few more episodes of *The Twilight Zone*.

DAY 2:

I've discovered that in kindergarten, there's a lot of repetition.

I've discovered that in kindergarten, there's a lot of repetition.

For instance, today Mrs. Ross wanted the kids to learn to push in their chairs when they got up from their tables to join her at the reading mat.

"Table One can join me on the mat. Gracie, push in your chair."

"That's good."

"All the way in."

"Even farther."

"Push it in a little more."

"Even farther."

"All the way in."

"Jonathan, no, we're not bringing our chairs with us."

"Yes, I know Miss Coffman is bringing her chair. But she's too big to sit on the floor. So, she can bring her chair."

"Charles, get down off your chair."

"Chip, don't push the chair in when Charles is standing on it."

"Miss Coffman, would you go pick up Charles?"

DAY 3

My typical stint is for an hour -- from 9:00 a.m. to 10:00 a.m. One hour is my limit. And I'm usually exhausted by the time I leave.

Today the kids were particularly rambunctious. I helped with breakfast, sang the alphabet song, took the kids to the bathroom, cleaned up spills, and chased after the kids who had wandered off from the reading mat. I knew I was helping, and I was glad to be there, but it suddenly hit me that I was tired.

Thank goodness it was almost time for me to leave.

I sneaked a peak at my watch.

It was only 9:10. I'd only been there ten minutes.

DAY 4

Today the kids were even more rambunctious than they were yesterday. By ten after 9:00, even Mrs. Ross was sneaking a peek at her watch.

DAY 5

Today Mrs. Ross taught the kids what to do when there was a fire drill. The girls were to go to the door and form a line. The boys were to go to the door and form a second line. Then both lines were to follow her outside to the playground.

The first few times they tried it, there were boys in the girls' line, and girls in the boys' line.

Obviously we have to start with the basics.

DAY 6

Today I found a little boy curled up under one of the tables.

Do you suppose he's been there for the past week and we just haven't noticed?

DAY 7

The kids were *really* rambunctious again today. I stayed an extra ten minutes to help out. Then I gathered my water bottle and keys.

After being with the kids, I needed to go to a warm, loving, safe environment – with adults.

"I have to go to Macy's," I explained to Mrs. Ross on my way out.

"Oh, do you *work* at Macy's?" She asked.

"No," I said. "I just have to go there."

DAY 9

I was telling my friend Rena about Kindergarten Camp. She told me about the time she paid for her granddaughter, Carley, to go to a similar pre-kindergarten program.

There's no fee for the program I've been helping out with, but there *was* for the program Rena sent Carley to.

Carley went with her when she wrote the check. But the more Carley thought about it, the less convinced she was that she was going to like it.

When Rena went to pick Carley up after the first day, Carley got into the car and buckled her seatbelt. Rena could tell she was not happy.

"You can go get your check back," Carley said. "I've learned all I need to learn."

DAY 10

I have now sung the alphabet song 10 days in a row.

A for apple -- a, a, a

B for bounce – b, b, b, b, b

C for cut – k, k, k

D for dig – d, d, d

Etc. etc. etc.

I don't sing it just at school. I sing it all day long. I can't get it out of my head.

Today, as I was singing it, when I got to the letter "L," I couldn't remember what "L" stood for. Liver?

27

Limestone? Liquid? Larry? Lollipop? Longtime? Liverwurst?

Lumpy? Looser? Lethargic? Loafer?

Lint? Linguist? Llama?

Left-handed?

So, I kept going back to the beginning and starting over, hoping that by the time I got to "L," I'd remember what it stood for. If I can't stop singing this song, I'm going to call Mrs. Ross at home to find out what "L" stands for, so I can get it out of my head.

DAY 11

"L" stands for "love."

The kids were especially energetic today. I stayed an extra ten minutes to help, then picked up my keys and said goodbye to Mrs. Ross. In fact, today I SANG goodbye to Mrs. Ross:

"I am leaving, L, L, L ."

Mrs. Ross sang back: "You are lucky, L, L, L, L."

DAY 12

Two big successes today. One little boy, who has yet to talk, seems to be following along . . . I think.

Every day when we sang the song about how to make the first ten numerals, I would take his arm and help him make the numerals in the air.

Today I wasn't close to where he was standing, but I looked over, and he was making the numerals with his arm all by himself!

Also, the boy who's been spending his time wandering around the room pretending he's an airplane sat down with us all and sang EVERY SONG – word for word. He's been listening all this time. Go figure.

DAY 13

I've become boring. I went out with my friends last night, and the only thing new in my life was the alphabet song. I sang it to them, but they only wanted to hear it once. They said they got it the first time through.

There's not a lot you can discuss about the alphabet song. I mean, you can't really have an in-depth discussion about why the word "apple" was chosen to represent the letter "A."

DAY 14

When I came in today, I discovered we were going to be using glue sticks again. That meant another load of washing tonight.

Amidst the stickiness, I asked myself: "Am I making a difference? *My* forte is teaching college freshmen to read between the lines. *That's* what I should be doing." And then I thought:

But to read between the lines, you have to know how to read.

And before you can learn to read, you have to learn the letters of the alphabet.

And before you can learn the alphabet, you have to learn to use a glue stick.

So, yes, I guess I'm making a difference.

DAY 15

Our last day. The parents were all invited today to graduation. They stood around the sides of the room, with their pre-kindergartener's brothers and sisters, shooting videos on their cell phones.

Mrs. Ross gathered the kids around her on the reading mat (well, all except for the airplane kid who had a meltdown and had to go home early with his mother) and they sang all the songs they'd learned.

William, who'd been (let's say) "overactive" all three weeks, sat on the floor like a little angel while his parents videotaped him. I couldn't believe it! What a stinker!

And Mrs. Ross was pretty funny, too. While she handed out their certificates for attending the camp, she said something positive about each of the kids.

"Oh, Mikey. I really enjoyed having you in class this summer!"

Was she kidding? *Mikey*? Mikey was an even bigger stinker than William was!

Hopefully Mikey's parents didn't see my face when she praised him.

After Mrs. Ross had spoken to each child and handed them their certificates, we had chocolate chip cookies and exchanged hugs and goodbyes.

On my way out, Pam asked me if I'd help out again next summer.

Why not?

The glue surely will have come out of my clothes by then.

And I'll have a lot more *Twilight Zones* under my belt.

Midwest Girl Finds Bra in New York

NEWS FLASH: West Lafayette, IN

It has just been revealed that Midwest teacher, writer, actress Sara Jane Coffman has found a bra that fits. A specialty shop near Times Square in New York recently successfully fitted Ms. Coffman. Women across the country who have been following Sara Jane's lifelong quest to find a comfortable bra are both stunned, and relieved.

The following is a transcript of the interview our reporter conducted with Ms. Coffman. The interview sheds light on the mystery of why she could never find a bra that fit . . . and how that mystery got solved.

Reporter: I understand you've never been able to find a bra that fit. Is that right?

SJC: That's right. I've tried everything! Nothing fit. The thing is, I've always slept on my stomach, so my breasts are under my armpits. And now that I've gotten older, my breasts have fallen down towards my waist.

Reporter: (Thinking that maybe his boss should have sent a female to conduct the interview): So, you ended up in New York City?

SJC: Yes, I was in New York City on a Road Scholar trip, and I happened to mention my problem to our program coordinator. I told her I'd even written a book called: *There's No Such Thing as a Comfortable Bra.*

She told me she had just the place for me. An exclusive little shop near Times Square that fits brides and Broadway actresses. She said, though, that I might not be able to get in. You need to have an appointment. She pulled out her cell phone and found the address and phone number for me. I called, and they were able to get me in!

Reporter: Were you apprehensive about going there?

SJC: For sure! But I checked their website before I went, and the owner seemed to have a good sense of humor. She said she had a Ph.D. in underwear. And she didn't have "salesladies." She had "Fairy Bra Mothers."

Reporter: Interesting. So how did you get to your appointment?

SJC: I walked from our hotel. Everyone else in our group was off sightseeing, so I went there on my own. It wasn't that hard. The streets of New York are laid out on a grid. I was looking for Ninth Avenue. The place was on Ninth Avenue.

It was an old building. There was a small lobby with a turn style in the middle of the room with little doors, waist-high. You had to go through the doors of the turn style to get to the elevators. So, I walked up and pushed on the little doors. They didn't move. I pushed harder. They didn't move.

No one was around. So, I began looking for a button on top of the turn style to push. I couldn't find one. I felt along the side of the turn style for a button to push. Couldn't find one. I tried pushing the little doors again. They didn't move.

Then a young man entered the building and sailed through the turn style next to mine. He went and stood at the elevator. So, I called out: "Excuse me. How did you get in?" And he held up a little ticket and said: "Use your pass."

Well, I didn't have a pass. He disappeared into the elevator.

Then I heard a loud voice behind me. A doorman was standing behind a desk. (Where was he when I came in?) He called me over and said: "Lady, what are you doing in this building?"

I got flustered and couldn't think of the name of the store, so I just said: "I'm here to buy a bra!"

"Sixth floor," he said, not sharing in the least my excitement about being there.

He must have buzzed me in or something because this time the little doors opened when I pushed.

I took the elevator to the sixth floor. Well, after my long walk from the hotel, and my nervousness about the fitting, I needed to go to the ladies' room. The good news was: I found it. The bad news was: It was locked.

So, then I went to find my exclusive little shop. There was no one in the hallway. The doors to all of the other stores (or offices?) were made out of metal with little windows at about the top of my head. I found my shop and tried the door. It was locked. I saw a button to push. I pushed the button. Then I tried the door. Then I read the sign on the door that read: "Don't push on the door. We'll come and get you."

I rose up on my toes to try to see in. A lady called out that she'd be right there. She came, opened the door, and invited me in. And then asked if I'd like to use the ladies' room.

Yes! So, she handed me a bra with a key card (like for your hotel room) on the end and told me the ladies' room was down the hall.

I really didn't want to carry a bra around with me out in the hallway, but I did.

Got to the ladies' room (still no one around) and put the key card up against the sensor on the wall to release the door. Nothing happened. I tried the door. It was locked. I tried the key again. Then I tried the door. I had visions of being stuck in the hallway forever.

35

Then, miraculously, a woman came out. I told her I'd been trying to get in but couldn't. Instead of opening the door further and letting me in, she came out, shut the door, and said: "I'll show you how to do it."

I didn't want a lesson! I wanted to go to the bathroom! She explained that the trick to that particular door was that you had to push hard. I hadn't been pushing hard enough.

I thanked her, entered the ladies' room, and did my thing.

I went back and buzzed to get back into the shop.

Reporter: Can you describe the shop?

SJC: Well, there was a tiny waiting room where Vera (she introduced herself as Vera) told me to have a seat. I sat on a dainty little loveseat, but there were also two dainty little chairs, and a small table with bridal magazines. The ceiling had exposed pipes.

A bride was paying her bill for the bra she bought and for all of the bras she had bought for her bridesmaids. The saleslady behind the desk was asking lots of questions about the wedding – it sounded like it was going to be quite an elaborate affair. And there I was, a tourist from Indiana, hoping to just find a comfortable bra.

When Vera finished with the bride, she took me back to a small room where there was a chair, and she pulled a flimsy little curtain closed. There seemed to be only one other saleslady in the store, and no other customers. Well, there may have been another one, but she must have been awfully quiet.

Vera asked me what I was looking for.

So I explained: "I'm looking for a bra that's *comfortable*."

"What size do you normally wear?"

"38B."

Then she looked at me – front and back – for about a second. She said she'd be right back.

And she returned with three possibilities. She began by telling me I should be wearing a size 32, not a 38.

Say what?

She had me bend forward and hooked the first bra behind my back. It had an underwire and two delicate little straps. When I turned around, she reached in and positioned my breasts into the cups. She called them my "ladies."

I told her that back in Indiana we call them "girls."

She replied (very tactfully) that she sometimes calls them "girls," too. But I felt special, knowing that in New York, I had "ladies," not "girls."

I looked in the mirror. Not only did the bra *look* good. It *felt* good! Every place it met my skin, it laid flat, like a glove.

I tried on the two other bras, but nothing came close to that first one. I tried on a bra with no underwire. Neither of us liked that. I tried on one with the cups trimmed in lace. We both agreed that wasn't me, either.

So, five minutes after I arrived, I exchanged my credit card for a sweet little bag containing my new bra and returned to my tour group. I showed it to all the women at dinner. They loved it!

Reporter: That's quite a story. Was it all worth it?

SJC: OMG! I've finally found a bra that fits! When I get up in the morning, I put it on, first thing. And I don't take it off until I go to bed. And throughout the day, I sometimes stop and think: Am I still wearing the bra?

Now, here's the best part. I read the tag when I got home. The name of the bra is "Chantelle." That's French! It's a *French* bra! All this time I've been trying to fit into *American* bras! There was no way they were going to fit. Not if I have French *breasts*!

So, now I'm thinking, maybe I should get DNA testing on the other parts of my body I'm having trouble with. Maybe some of my other body parts have different origins, too.

Reporter: Uh, huh. So, do you have any advice for our readers?

SJC: Sure! If you decide to go get fitted at this place, look for the doorman. He's a little scary, but you need him to get through the turn style.

Push *hard* on the door to the ladies' room.

And tell Vera I said "Hi!"

Just Deal With it
(And Other Reassuring Things Your
Mother Said to You)

My mother grew up during the depression and got married right at the start of WWII. After living through those two events, raising a family was a piece of cake. Nothing bothered her. In fact, her favorite saying was: "You're going to look back on this and laugh."

The problem was, as a teen-ager, I went from (what I thought was) one traumatic event to another, but my mother never let me wallow in them. She'd simply say: "You're going to look back on this and laugh." And she'd continue on with her ironing, or whatever it was she was doing.

At the time, it was rather annoying. I *wanted* to have a crisis. I *wanted* to wallow. As I got older, I realized that wasn't such a bad philosophy to have.

My mother had a number of sayings that I remember and that shaped my life. Which got me to thinking: What did other mothers say?

So, I began asking my friends: was there something your mom used to say to you that you remember, or that you've carried through your life, as words of wisdom? I got many of the same answers, like "Eat your vegetables," "Stand up straight," and "Put that back, you'll spoil your supper."

But here are some of the more unusual things people shared:

1. "What were you thinking?" (Kathy's mother said this, obviously when she'd done something stupid.)

2. "I told you that would happen." (Rhonda's mom said this, but everyone's mother probably thought it.)

3. "Read my lips." (Monica's mom used to say this. Sometimes, when Monica's mom told her to do something, Monica would question *why* she had to do it. Her mom would simply say: "Read my lips.")

4. Gretchen's older sisters told her: "If you can't be good, be careful." (A mother probably wouldn't have said that!)

5. "You're not going to Ft. Lauderdale for spring break." (Toni's mom said this for five years, while she was in college.)

6. My mother used to say: "If it was meant to be, it will be." (She usually said it whenever I was complaining that I wasn't getting something I wanted.)

7. "Get out and walk!" My friend Lisa used to say this when her four kids were fighting in the car. Lisa had four kids in four and a half years. (There was

one pair of twins.) Her daughter Angela said her mom would pull the car over and make them get out if they were within reasonable distance of their house. ("Reasonable" being a subjective term.) Angela said she'd get out, and usually the sibling she was fighting with would get out as well.

8. "He who sleeps late, hurries the rest of the day." (Martha's mother said this.)

9. "She can't help it, it's the way her mother puts her hat on." (This is from Diane's mother, a WWII British war bride. It was meant to excuse someone's poor behavior.)

10. "You make your bed, you sleep in it." (Monica's mother said this. The funny thing is, Monica took it literally. She thought her mother actually wanted her to make her bed, so she always did. When she got older, she realized it had to do with making good decisions, not making her bed.)

11. On Christmas Eve, when my mother tucked us in bed, she'd say: "Sleep fast." She probably wanted us to fall asleep quickly so she and my dad could assemble the presents under the tree. But I remember lying awake trying to figure out how to "sleep fast." (I now tell myself to "sleep fast" on Christmas Eve.)

12. When my friend Myra's son Mikey was acting up, she'd tell him "I'm going to count to 'one.' And I'd better not get there." Most mothers count to three, but Myra had her kids later in life and said she

didn't want to give them a chance to drive her nuts while she was still at "one" and "two."

13. "Mommy's tired, so it's time for you to go to bed." (Renee's mom never said this; it's what Renee used to say to her kids.)

14. "Don't get up until the clock says 8-0-0." (Amy's mom used to say this when she was little.)

15. "Well, what could POSSIBLY go wrong?" Myra said this when one of her kids was contemplating doing something stupid. (Must be said with appropriate sarcasm.)

16. "Make two trips." My mom said this, usually if I was trying to carry too much in my arms, and especially if something in the pile was breakable. I think about this now, though, in terms of trying to do too much. Sometimes I remind myself to mentally "make two trips."

17. "That's maid work." Well, I thought that's what my mother was saying. She said it when I was doing a chore she'd given me -- and I agreed with her: it *was* beneath me to have to do it. We should get a maid to do it.

But what she meant was: "That's MADE work." You made things worse than what they were. For example, one time I was mad about having to mop the kitchen floor, and in the middle of that task, I knocked over the bucket of dirty water. My mother heard the crash, came into the kitchen, and declared that I had just made "made" work.

At the time our mothers imparted their wisdom, their sayings may have seemed a bit harsh. But most of them were designed to point out our mistakes and keep us from making the same mistakes in the future. For example, the next time it was my turn to mop the kitchen floor, I was a lot more careful when I moved the bucket of water.

Some of our mothers' sayings were philosophies to help us deal with life. For example: "If that's the worst thing that happens to you, you're in good shape." Our mothers were trying to tell us that there were going to be things in our lives that we wouldn't be able to control . . . or that wouldn't make sense. If something like that happened, we should let it go and move on.

And, lastly, some of the sayings brought us comfort. "There's always tomorrow" meant "I know what you're going through" and "You're going to get through this."

Whether they were pointing out our flaws, giving us philosophies to help us deal with life, or comforting us, our mothers were keeping an eye on us and helping us grow.

God bless them.

The Older I Get, The Smarter My Mother Was

I have a strange and bizarre story in my head about my mother's birth. I want to say it was my mom who told me, and it must have been, because no one else in the family has ever heard it. They think I made it up.

The story was, my grandmother gave birth in the kitchen in her farmhouse. This was during the depression. There was no doctor available (my grandparents lived in the country), so my grandfather got the closest thing he could – a WWI medic who performed a C-section on my grandmother there on the kitchen table.

The part of the story that *has* been confirmed by the family is that my grandmother was very weak for the following two years. Her three sisters took turns coming over and taking care of the baby.

And my grandmother never had any more children.

My mother was never an outwardly affectionate person, and I attribute that to my story of her birth – that she didn't receive as much hugging and affection as other babies do.

My mother grew up on a farm, and quickly decided that wasn't the lifestyle she wanted. From an early age, she was in charge of going out to the barn and wringing the chicken's neck when they were having chicken that night for dinner. After she left home, she avoided chickens, and rarely ate chicken or served it to us.

Growing up, she loved to learn and excelled in school. In high school, she was an accomplished pianist and earned money by accompanying professional singers. I have some of her piano music and it's incredibly complicated.

She wanted to go to college which, at the time, wasn't possible. My grandfather did agree to send her to beauty school with the condition that she'd remain in their small town for a year afterwards, which she did. But when that year was up, she was off to the big city. In Cleveland, she roomed with three other young girls. According to my dad, one of the roommates was a bit on the wild side. The story was she'd been known to greet her second date of the evening at the front door while her roommates were escorting her first date out the back. I don't know if all three of the girls did that, or if it was just that one.

My parents were on their honeymoon in Washington D.C. when the U.S. declared war on Germany and Japan. During the war, my dad taught navigation classes for Naval officers and my mom was a code breaker. She never talked about her work, but she was a whiz at solving problems and figuring out puzzles. When my brother and sister and I were growing up, she was constantly entering contests and winning toys, bicycles, roller skates, cowboy sets, and dolls. She even helped me win a purebred Siamese kitten. (Which my dad was not too thrilled about.)

For what she may have lacked in hugging skills, she made up for in managerial skills. Which she needed since my dad traveled. She ran the house, cooked the meals, took us shopping, drove us to school when we missed the bus, and entertained my dad's colleagues when he brought them home for dinner at the last minute.

She took the car in for servicing and arranged for the home repairs when something in the house broke down. She took us to boy scouts, brownies, piano lessons, ballet lessons, and swimming lessons.

She was politically-minded and worked the polls on election days. For several different censuses, she went door-to-door, interviewing the residents.

She had a chemistry lab in the basement and I'd watch her mix chemicals together to get stains out of our clothes. To save money, she ironed my dad's white shirts on a big mangle iron. She sewed costumes for me when I was in plays at school and made beautiful dresses for me to wear to dances.

She never swore. (Although she could give you a look that would wither you.) Also, if she was displeased with you, she would sniff. You always knew you were in trouble when she sniffed.

She had interesting things to say, so she never had to gossip. (At least, I never heard her.) When one of her girlfriends came over for coffee, we kids were banished to another room. Or better yet, outdoors, so they could talk. That's the line I remember my mother saying to us the most: "Go out and play." It could have been raining or snowing, but if my mother wanted us out of the house, we got out.

Maybe that's how she kept the house so clean.

My mother instilled in us a love of books. From the time we were little, she took my brother and sister and me on the city bus across town to the public library. I think the first few times I just sat on the floor of the library, bored. That didn't faze my mother. She knew that eventually I'd start to read, and I did.

My most precious memories of my mom are when I'd come home from school and tell her about my day. She saved her ironing or sorting the clothes for that time so she could sit and listen.

She was both feminine and a feminist. She wore dresses, not pants. She wore makeup when she and my dad went out. And when I was old enough, she sent me downtown to Higbee's Charm School so I could learn the proper way to put on makeup, too.

And she was a feminist long before that word was every invented.

There were two things my mom did that were really quite clever. One was, she had a rule that if there was ever a fight, the oldest child was the one who'd get punished. It didn't matter whose fault it was. The oldest child should have known better. It would have been either my brother or me who got punished. I don't remember any fights at our house.

The other clever thing was the way she handled shopping. When there was a sale, she would take my brother to the sale first and leave my sister and me at home. When they returned, my brother would jump out of the car (with his new shoes, or whatever) and I would jump in. You knew to be ready. If you weren't ready, you'd miss your turn.

In rearing us, my parents always put up a united front. My dad's mantra was: "Whatever your mother says, goes."

She was a skilled photographer, wonderful at framing a shot. For years she developed her pictures in a makeshift dark room in the basement. She left my brother and sister and me a legacy of thousands of photos that she took as we were growing up. I wonder if she knew at the time the treasure she was leaving us.

My sister has scanned those slides into the computer and I've spent many happy hours looking at them. There was one photo that I particularly treasure.

I'd been writing a story about when I was a little girl and how my parents took me to an amusement park and put me in one of those little boats that goes around in a pool of water.

Truth be told, I didn't really remember that ever happening. I was pretty sure that I could just be making it up. But then I ran across the photo. There I was – about age two – wearing a little pink coat and a little pink hat that tied under my chin. I was sitting with my brother in a red metal boat at an amusement park.

When I asked my cousin Margie what she remembered about my mom, she said: "We always had fun when your mom was around!" My mother had a great sense of fun and sense of humor. On our summer camping trips, she was always coming up with neat places to visit and things to do. The most memorable experience was the time she, my dad, my Aunt Margaret, and my Uncle Jim were sharing our tent. The four of us cousins were sent to the station wagon to sleep. Well, we were supposed to sleep, but the adults in the tent were laughing so hard all night, we couldn't.

When she was getting ready for bed, my mother discovered that of the two pairs of pajamas she'd packed for the trip, she'd only packed the tops. No bottoms. The four adults giggled about that all night.

My mother was fearless. One story that comes to mind is the time my grandparents came to visit us when we were living in New Jersey. My dad worked for the

Erie Lackawanna Railroad, and we had free passes to take the train into New York City. So, my mom decided that she and I would take her parents for a visit to New York.

My mom had me drop the three of them off at the train station so they wouldn't have so far to walk, and she told me to go park the car and then hurry back to meet them to catch the train. Well, something must have been going on in town that day, and I couldn't find a parking spot. I finally found one, but it was nowhere near the train station. I ran back to the station as fast as I could.

There was my mother -- holding the train. She was standing with one foot on the step of the train and one foot on the platform. The conductor was pleading with her to board the train – that it was going to leave, but she wouldn't budge until she got her daughter safely on board.

She was only five foot one, but she held that train until I got there.

My mother loved the theatre and instilled in me *my* love of the theatre. My dad was not so enamored. The agreement she and my dad had is that he'd take her to any play or concert she wanted, as long as she'd let him sleep through it.

After she and my dad put their three kids through college, my mom went back to school and got her degree.

In her later years, my mother spent her days doing difficult crossword puzzles and reading books. She was always reading. I think she was trying to keep her brain active, but in the long run, Alzheimer's caught up with her. I read somewhere that people who develop Alzheimer's are people who don't want to die. And this might have been true for my mother. She truly enjoyed her life. She had fun. She was talented and skilled, and she had a lifetime of accomplishments.

My father was devoted to her for sixty-five years. After she passed, I asked him how he was dealing with her being gone. He told me that he still woke up at night and heard her calling him from her bedroom down the hall.

He'd call back: "I'm coming, Dorothy."

And when he passed, he kept that promise.

Poem to My Mother

I wrote this poem to cheer my mother up when she came home from a shopping trip and told us she'd just hit a truck. My dad, brother, sister, and I spilled out into the driveway to look at the damage. The car was drivable, but the right front end was bashed in. She'd smashed it when pulling around a delivery truck that was parked in the middle of the street!

We hugged her, and laughed, and told her that cars can be fixed; we were just glad that she was O.K. But it was a while before she laughed at my poem.

Ode to Mom on Hitting a Truck

It was a dark and stormy night
(Actually, it was sunny, there, and bright)

When Dorothy Mae, she ventured out
A library book she wanted.
But lo and behold, she met a TRUCK!
That's how her front end got bended.

Her husband, he did laugh
(And so did her daughter)

It was time you hit *something*
The odds say you oughtta.

Twas just a nick! The family all cried.
But wouldn't you know it, it hurted her pride.

You've got to get over it
Macy's is calling
If you choose not to drive
To the mall you'll be crawling.

Everyone hits something
But you hit a TRUCK!
We're proud of you, mom
It shows you have pluck!

We'll be telling this story
Ages and ages hence
Two vehicles converged in the road
And hurt was the truck, not the fence.

I Write Good Thank You Notes

If there's one thing I do well, it's write good thank you notes. From the time I was in her womb, my mother made me sit down the day after Christmas and write thank you notes for the presents people had given me. So, I got into the habit of writing thank you notes early on.

The formula for writing a thank you note is simple: You start with the key elements – state exactly what the present was, express delight over receiving it, tell how you're going to use it (or, better yet, how you've already used it), and finish off with a comment about how much the present means to you.

Even though I have the *ability* to write good thank you notes, it takes me a long time to write one, so it's not my favorite thing to do.

The thing I like best about thank you notes is that it's the one time in the world when you can lie. As long as you're sincere, it's perfectly acceptable to lie in a thank you note.

And sometimes people should lie. For instance, a colleague of mine at work should have lied the other day when I gave her a book I knew she'd like for her birthday. I'd gone clear across town on a Friday night

– in rush hour – to get the only copy there was of this book. It was a hard-back, and it cost a pretty penny. But I'd thought about it a great deal and knew she'd enjoy it.

When I gave it to her, she said, in a rather bored voice, "Oh, I've already read this." And she put it aside. I desperately wanted to ask: "Well, then, can I have it back?"

She should have either given it back, or just thanked me and left out the part about already having read it.

My writing great thank you notes finally came back to haunt me. The other day, a woman in the locker room at my gym who I know casually, complimented me on my outfit. Then she said she had a bag of clothes in the trunk of her car that were too small for her daughter that were probably my size. Would I like to have them? If I couldn't use them, I could do whatever I wanted with them, but she was I sure I'd love them.

Now, I like to buy my own clothes, but the lady looked like she really wanted me to have them. So, after our exercise class, I followed her out to the parking lot and lugged the huge bag full of clothes from her car to mine.

When I got home, I went through them. There were skirts, dresses, pants, and tops. My eyes lit up when I looked at the tags. They were all high-level, name brands, like Talbot's, B. Moss, and Banana Republic! I just won the lottery!

Unfortunately, none of the clothes fit. Nor were they my style. But they were all beautiful, expensive clothes. What was I going to do with them?

Aha. I'd take them to the local Consignment Shop and sell them. And make some extra money! Our Consignment Shop is very particular about the clothing they accept, so I decided to wash everything. I wanted to be careful, so instead of using my regular laundry detergent, I decided to use a gentler one. I didn't have a gentler one. I made a trip to the grocery to get a small bottle of gentle laundry detergent. They didn't have a small bottle. Well, this was an investment, I thought. I bought the large bottle.

I spent the day carefully washing and ironing the clothes and hanging them on hangers. All the time excited about the easy money that was going to come my way.

I loaded the clothes into my car and drove across town to the Consignment Shop. I waited for them to look the clothes over and hand me my contract. Waited. And waited. And waited. Eventually, one of the ladies who worked there came over to me (I'd been sitting there reading a book) and told me that they'd finished looking through my clothes a long time ago.

So, I closed my book and went to the front desk. To hear the bad news. They were only going to accept two of the twenty-five items. They handed me back the rest of the clothes.

I didn't ask what was wrong with the clothes they didn't accept. With my head held high, I proudly lugged them back to my car.

Now what was I going to do with them? They were not styles that the young girls were wearing, or else I could have taken them to the local high school where there's a "closet" where the students can shop for free.

I showed them to a group of friends at lunch. Would anyone like them? No. Did they have any suggestions for what I could do with them? Not really.

I didn't want to take them home. I didn't want to keep them in my car. I ended up taking them to Goodwill.

I returned home and spent the afternoon writing a thank you note to the lady who'd given me the clothes, telling her how much I was going to enjoy them.

The only thing I was "out" was the time I'd spent washing and ironing the clothes, the time I'd spent at the Consignment Shop and Goodwill, the time I'd spent writing the thank you note, and the money for the expensive laundry detergent.

End of story.

The next week, when I arrived at the gym, the woman who'd given me the clothes hurried over to me and thanked me profusely for my lovely thank you note.

I told her no problem. My pleasure.

Then she said: "Since you liked the clothes so much, I brought you another bag. It's in my car."

All I could think to say was: "Did you keep the thank you note?"

High School Band Parents

I grew up in a suburb of Cleveland, Ohio. In my high school, the big thing was wrestling. Our wrestling coach had seven sons – all spread out in age– and we were the state wrestling champions for decades.

When I moved to Indiana, it didn't take long to realize the state sport is football.

Not pro ball.

Not college ball.

High school football.

During the fall, high school football dominates the newspaper headlines and television newscasts. Stores display posters of the players in their front windows. On Fridays, everyone wears the school colors. You can always rely on high school football if you want to start up a conversation with someone in a doctor's waiting room or in line at the grocery.

The proudest people in town, though, are not the parents of the football players. They're the parents of the kids in the marching band.

In fact, in the story I'm about to tell you, the band parents were the wildest and craziest group of people

I've ever run across – both on a football field or in the stands.

I had heard about the band parents' section of the bleachers here in West Lafayette and decided I should experience it first-hand. So, armed with a pen and pad of paper, I went to a game and positioned myself (undercover) in the band parent section.

It was like being at a huge family reunion. The women hugged the other parents as they arrived, and the men high-fived each other. While they were staking out their seats and unpacking their coolers, everyone talked to everyone. There seemed to be no secrets. Everyone knew whose kid was dating whom, who had broken up with whom, who was going to the dance, and what the latest terrible assignment was in social studies.

While all this information was being exchanged, out came the food. People passed out sandwiches, calling out the different selections. The hotdog vendor came around and filled hotdog orders. Soft drinks squirted open. Popcorn was spilled all over as the littler kids tried to open the bags themselves.

I think the game might have started, but there was too much activity in our section to have noticed.

Everyone had to shout to be heard because we were sitting right next to the band, and they were loud. It might have been my imagination, but it felt as if the trumpets, trombones, and percussion instruments aimed their music at us, and not at the field. It was a warm evening, so every so often, when a band member needed a drink of water, a parent (not necessarily his or hers) would jump up and take them some water.

This chaos continued through the first half of the game. Then suddenly, it was the event the parents had all been waiting for.

Half-time.

Half-time is special because that's when some of the fathers help the band transport their instruments to the fifty-yard line for their half-time show. To prepare for this event, those fathers stood up, did some stretches and deep knee bends, and hiked their pants up.

Their wives hugged them proudly as if they were sending them off to war.

I'll admit, it was no small feat moving marimbas, tympanies, vibraphones and xylophones from the sideline quickly onto the field, especially considering that those instruments were on wheels and had to be rolled across wet grass.

But the fathers moved like a well-oiled machine. Each one knew where they were going, and what they had to do. They reminded me of the pit crews at a NASCAR race.

There was only one small crisis. A wheel on the xylophone fell off, and the father in charge of pushing it had to stop and put it back on.

Once the instruments were in place, the husbands ran off the field, wildly waving their arms and shouting to their wives. The wives wildly waved and shouted back to their husbands. It looked like a scene from a movie – both sides yelling and waving to each other. There was more cheering for the husbands than for any of the touchdowns made by either of the teams.

I'm not sure how much football the band – or the band parents – saw. In fact, I overheard one band member say to another: "Hey, why did we just play that song?" ("Our" team had just scored a touchdown.)

If you haven't been to a local high school football game recently, you should go. It's a great way to spend a Friday evening. There's plenty of fresh air, hotdogs, cheering, and good fun.

And if you sit in the band parents' section, you'll get to see first-hand how enormously proud the band parents are of their kids.

At the end of the evening, when I was there, we all left with big smiles because our team had won.

But on our way out of the stadium, I overheard a band parent ask: "Does anyone know what team we just played?"

My Latest Air Travel Adventure

I recently visited New York City. I hadn't flown in a while and I'd never flown to NYC before, so when making my plane reservations, I had to decide which airport I wanted to fly into. I had three choices: JFK, LaGuardia, or Newark. Knowing nothing about any of those airports, I selected LaGuardia since it had a flight that left Indianapolis around the noon hour. That way I'd have plenty of time to get to the airport, and plenty of time to enjoy New York once I arrived.

I got to the Indianapolis airport with enough time to sit down and have a nice breakfast. While sitting there, I observed a very professionally-dressed woman sitting at the table next to mine. She was with her husband and her one-year-old twins who were in a deluxe, double stroller. I chuckled to myself when I heard her order "The Overachiever."

I thought that was fitting.

When I went through security, the TSA guys called me "Miss" and "Young Lady." I loved it! To all the men reading this, those little words mean a lot to us "older gals." I had a spring in my step as I picked my bag off the conveyer belt and headed to my gate.

While waiting for my flight, I was wonderfully amused by listening to two young men talking about their wives. I don't think either of them had been married very long. They exchanged stories about their wives not understanding things about owning a house that seemed obvious to them. One man said his wife wanted him to rent a machine to chip a huge tree stump out of the back yard. He said it took a long time to explain to her that that was the kind of job you called in a professional to do. (He obviously had no intention of removing the stump himself.) His friend nodded in sympathy and solidarity.

Neither of the men said anything negative or disparaging about their wives. They just seemed baffled about having to explain things to their wives that were perfectly obvious to them.

The airline employee at the counter at our gate got on the P.A. system and announced that our flight was full and that it was doubtful we'd all be able to take our carry-ons on board. She asked us to voluntarily check our bags with her – especially if they were oversized.

I was a bit concerned about the size of my carry-on, even though I'd taken it on flights before and knew it fit under the seat in front of me. I looked around at the other travelers. On the floor directly in front of me was a HUGE carry-on. Surely, they weren't going to let that on. Then I looked up at the bag's owner. He was scowling and had his arms crossed defiantly in front of him. I decided to stand behind him in line so that my carry-on and I wouldn't look so bad.

When it was getting close to the time to board, I decided it was time to hit the ladies' room. With my right hand, I rolled my carry-on into the ladies' room. My backpack and ticket were in my left hand. I wanted to check my teeth in the mirror – I didn't want to arrive in New York with food stuck in my teeth. I took my glasses off, held them in my right hand, and leaned over the sinks to look in the mirror. Suddenly, my glasses started filling with soap! Inadvertently, I'd triggered the automatic soap dispenser when I leaned in to look at my teeth!

It took my brain forever to figure out what was happening. By the time I figured out I should step back from the mirror, my glasses were covered with about a half an inch of soap.

So, there I was holding my soapy glasses with my right hand, and my backpack and ticket in my left. There was no ledge on which to set my glasses. I had no idea where the nearest paper towel dispenser was because I didn't have my glasses on. Then I heard them calling my flight. I wiped the soap off on my sweatshirt and pants and got in line to board.

Once I boarded, it was just a short trip – an hour and half from Indy to LaGuardia. There was a lot of turbulence, but I assured myself that nobody ever died from turbulence. They may have been freaked out, but they didn't die of turbulence.

We landed safely. All-in-all, it was a safe and uneventful flight. My time in New York was wonderful and before I knew it I was headed back home.

When I returned to LaGuardia airport for my flight back home, I had a good look at the airport. It was the most decrepit, run-down, dilapidated airport I've ever seen. On the bright side, they must have been trying to correct that because there was a lot of construction going on. On the not-so-bright side, some of the large equipment was stuck in huge mud puddles and police were standing in the rain directing traffic. Some of the lanes – some of the IMPORTANT lanes – like "departing flights" were blocked off.

I bought some cute little tuna bites at their convenience store and found a seat, which was not an easy thing to do, since it was lunch hour, and the airport was packed.

Then I had a problem: I couldn't get the plastic container open. It said: "Push" on two tabs, and "Pull" on two other tabs. I pushed and pulled for about ten minutes. I was going to have to get someone to help me, but I didn't want to relinquish my valuable seat. People whizzed by, pulling their carry-ons and talking on their cell phones, but nobody looked friendly enough to ask them to stop and help. Eventually I found an older guy who was waiting tables across the concourse and waved at him to please come over and help me open my lunch. He had no trouble at all opening the package.

When it was time to board, I saw that my boarding pass said: Zone 3. At first, I didn't know what that meant. Then it became apparent.

First, the Premium passengers board. Then the Priority passengers. Then the First-class passengers. Then Zone 1 passengers, Zone 2 passengers, and finally Zone 3 passengers. By the time Zone 3 passengers board, there's not going to be any space left in the overhead bins, so Zone 3 passengers have to surrender their bags. Basically, Zone 3 passengers are scum.

There's no hiding the fact that you're in Zone 3. You're the ones with no carry-on bags, relegated to the back of the plane. You have to walk past everyone who's already settled in their seat. They look up at you with awkward little smiles, and you both know they're thinking that that's what we get for not paying as much money for our tickets as they did for theirs.

After giving it some thought, I've come up with what I think is a much better system for boarding.

I think airlines should board the people who are the most tired first.

That way I'd always get a good seat.

Playing Hide-And-Seek with My Cats

I have two Siamese cats who let me live with them, and they're as different as two people (or animals) could be.

Simba is the younger of the two. Of all the adjectives I could use to describe him, gifted would not be one of them. But he makes up for it by being excited about everything. To him, everything in life is exciting and fun.

"We're going to eat?" Yes!

"You're going to take a nap and I can sit on your lap?" Great!

"Hey, the sun's out! I can sit in the sun!"

Tuey, my older kitty, is much more laid back and has a much higher IQ. I've never had Tuey tested, but there's a good chance her IQ is higher than mine.

Tuey is an old soul. She and I can sit for long periods of time just looking at each other. When I look into her eyes there's such depth that I can see the beginning of time. Tuey knows everything.

And, being a Siamese cat, of course, she's very much her own person. She likes *me*, but I'm the only person she likes. She has no use for other people. She's also very careful about how she uses her time.

Simba, as you can imagine, likes everybody and is up for anything at any time.

The other day I was doing laundry in my basement and the two cats were sitting on the basement steps looking bored. So, I decided to hide behind the hot water heater that's in the middle of the room. Simba got curious, immediately followed behind me, and took great delight in "catching" up with me.

I circled around the hot water heater again as fast as I could and then ran and hid behind the furnace, which was also in the middle of the room. He followed behind and caught me again.

So, I ran around the hot water heater again. And we began playing hide-and-seek.

I'd stop and change directions. Sometimes I'd stop completely. Sometimes he'd jump up on the air filter on the furnace and cut me off at the pass – which I told him was cheating.

We had fun.

Later that day, when Simba was upstairs taking his nap, Tuey came down to the basement to watch me to put my clothes in the dryer. She probably could use some exercise, so I decided to play hide-and-seek with *her*. I moved behind the hot water heater.

Then moved to the furnace. Tuey doesn't move as quickly as Simba does, so I was way out in front of her. I hid behind the hot water heater again. I looked back. She hadn't caught up with me yet.

I circled the furnace.

Then circled the hot water heater.

She was *way* behind me.

I circled the furnace again.

And the hot water heater.

Still no cat.

Then I happened to look up.

There she sat.

At the top of the basement steps.

Just watching me.

On Getting Up in the Morning

When I was growing up, I don't think I ever asked my parents if I could stay up past my bedtime. After a hard day of playing, I was usually in bed fast asleep by the time my bedtime rolled around.

My best friend Vicki was even better at sleeping than I was. When I'd spend the night at her house, she'd begin telling me a story, fall asleep in the middle of a sentence, and wake up the next morning and finish the sentence.

Now that I'm older, to prepare for bed, I have an entire routine.

I begin by taking a hot bath with Epson salts which helps my sore knees and legs. Then I do a Sudoku puzzle, read a chapter from whatever book I'm reading, and listen to some quiet, relaxing music. Then I crawl into bed.

And arrange my pillows.

I begin by positioning a small pillow under my knees for when I lie on my back.

Then, I position two large, heavy pillows up against my right and left sides for when I sleep on my side and want to throw my top leg up and over.

Then I position a small, down-filled pillow under my head. I've had it for so long, and it's so old that I have to punch it a few times to get the feathers to go where I want them.

Thus barricaded, I put on a night mask to block out the light from the windows. Unable now to see, I reach over and grasp around to try to find the little metal pull-chain to turn off the light on the table next to my bed.

Then I say my prayers, clear my head, and drift off to sleep.

I wish.

Instead of drifting off to sleep, my analytical brain comes alive. Bedtime, my brain believes, is the perfect time for me to try to solve the world's problems. After trying, and realizing that I can't, I run through all the things I have planned to do the next day. And by then, I have to get up and go to the bathroom one more time.

I have no idea how it happens, but I start off positioned north and south in the bed all tightly tucked in like a swaddled newborn. I wake up in the morning in an east-west direction, at the foot of the bed, blankets tangled and askew, the pillows all on the floor.

And that's my typical nighttime routine.

Fast forward to the next morning. I also have a routine for getting *out* of bed. When I was younger, I used to simply get out of bed. Now that I'm older, first I have to check in with my body parts.

This morning, for example, I began by checking my breathing. Sometimes my sinuses clog up during the night. Yes, I was breathing.

Then I checked my right ear. Was it full of fluid from sleeping on my right side too long? Yes, it was. So, I tilted my head to the left until the fluid drained from my ear back into my head.

My next issue was with my right knee. My low impact aerobics class is fun, but it aggravates my knee. My knee indicated it was not happy with me. I promised it that if it helped me get up, I'd give it some glucosamine.

Then I checked in with my left shoulder, which I strained the other day carrying a 30-pound bag of kitty litter from the grocery store to the car, and then again from the car inside the house. How sore was it? Pretty sore. I must have slept too long on my left side.

After checking in with my body, I checked in with my brain. Was I going to be doing anything exciting today that I should start getting ready for? Not that I could think of.

Then I assessed things on my emotional front. Was I mad at anyone yesterday that I should remember to continue being mad at today?

By this time, I had to go to the bathroom. So, I sat up, swung my legs over the side of the bed, and dug around through the covers to try to find my socks (which I had carefully placed on the end of the bed so I could easily find them.) I bent my leg to put my first sock on.

My body instantly responded yelling: "TOO SOON! TOO SOON!" IT'S TOO SOON TO BE ASKING US TO BEND LIKE THAT!"

I foregoed (forewent?) putting on my shoes and socks. Barefooted, I went downstairs to the kitchen, hoping not to stub my toe on anything on my way. And hoping not to fall over the cats who were racing down the stairs ahead of me.

First things first. I opened a can of cat food and put it in their dish. Tuey looked at it and said: "Are you nuts? You know I won't eat that stuff. That's the cheap stuff."

"That's all I have. I need to go to the grocery."

She cocked her head. "I'll bet there's a can of tuna in the cupboard."

"You're not getting the tuna."

"Then go to the store."

"I'm not going to the store until later this morning."

She gave me a dirty look.

I gave her a dirty look back.

She threw her scarf over her shoulder dramatically and went back upstairs to bed.

Although my stomach had said it was ready for breakfast, my bones, joints, and muscles said they weren't moving until they got a hot shower. In the shower, I aimed the stream of hot water on my shoulders and stood there until my muscles began to loosen up. Slowly, the hot water relaxed my joints and I could begin moving them again. I felt like how the Tin Man must have felt when Dorothy oiled him.

Time to get dressed. Aha! Now, *there* was something pleasant to look forward to. I could wear my new, really comfortable jeans that I bought last week at Macy's.

What made them so comfortable was the wide, elastic waistband. It was the first time I'd seen a pair of jeans with such a nice, wide, elastic waistband. It wasn't until I got them home and read the tag that I discovered they were maternity pants. I probably should have returned them, but they were *really* comfortable.

Finally, it was time for breakfast. What was I hungry for? Scrambled eggs would be good. No, I'd have to wash the pan first.

Oatmeal would be good. But I was out of milk.

I settled for a banana.

Thus cleansed, dressed, and fed, there was only one more thing to do.

Go back upstairs and make my bed . . . . so I could do the whole thing over again tonight.

My Most Wonderful Nap

Not only do I enjoy sleeping, I enjoy taking naps. And the other day I had the best nap I've ever had in my life.

You know the kind I'm talking about. It's where you're sitting in a chair watching TV or reading a book, and your head starts falling forward towards your lap.

And when your head is almost to your lap, and it's beginning to be uncomfortable, you straighten back up and go back to watching TV or reading your book. But pretty soon your head starts falling forward towards your lap again.

And when it becomes truly uncomfortable, you lift your head back up and straighten your spine to sit back up again. When you can't fight it any longer, your head falls back into your lap.

I was having that kind of nap.

But then, for some reason, at one of the times when I straightened up, I glanced over at Sam who was sitting next to me and saw that his eyes were closed and that he was sound asleep.

Interesting.

So, then I looked over at our friend Chuck who was sitting next to him and saw that he, too, was sound asleep.

What was going on?

Then it hit me.

We were in church.

Couldn't Get My Sweatshirt On

Last night I woke up in the middle of the night and had to go to the bathroom. The thing is, my bedroom is upstairs and my bathroom is downstairs. I was going to have to go downstairs.

The trick was going to be staying only partially awake so I could get back to sleep easily when I got back upstairs.

My plan was working. I successfully navigated the stairs – in the dark – without falling. Successfully made it to the bathroom – still in the dark. Then I felt a little chilled, so before I went back upstairs, I decided to put my sweatshirt on.

Again, without turning any lights on, I carefully felt my way into my study to get the sweatshirt that I keep on the back of my computer chair.

I found the sweatshirt and inserted my left arm into the sleeve. I found the right sleeve and inserted my right arm. But I could NOT find the opening for my head.

I started over. Right arm in one sleeve. Left arm in the other. I still couldn't find the opening for my head.

Frustrated, I turned the bright, overhead light on.

And saw the problem.

I'd been trying to get into my sweatpants.

Burning Questions for Which I Am Seeking Answers

1. Why do my Siamese cats shed their dark-brown hair on my white clothes, and their white hair on my dark clothes?

2. Why do my cats throw up in the middle of my queen-size Laura Ashley comforter instead of on the hardwood floor, where it would be easy to clean up?

3. Why is my phone always in the other room?

4. Why do some of my friends have their birthdays on the first day of the month when they know I won't see it until I turn the page of my calendar and then it's too late to send them a card?

5. Why is it cold in church when I forget to bring a "wrap," and hot when I've chosen to wear a pull-over sweater?

6. Why is it always pouring rain -- or blizzarding -- on the day my library books are due?

7. Why do so many people go to the grocery store at the same time *I* want to?

8. Why don't I fill my car with gas before I desperately need it and the temperature has fallen to 17 below?

9. Why is it that you go for a long time with nothing to do, and then there are two things you want to do that are scheduled for the exact same time?

10. Why is it that no matter what size bag you buy, there's never as much top soil as you need?

11. Why do dresses look better on the hanger than they do on me?

12. Why, in his fall newsletter, did the mayor of West Lafayette urge us to celebrate the fact that we have four seasons? Is he nuts? We don't have four seasons! We have only a few days of spring, and a few days of fall. Oh, wait. I get it! We *do* have four seasons: Cold. *Miserably* cold. Hot. And *miserably* hot. (Seriously – I love this town. I'm just a little nuts when it comes to the weather.)

13. Why didn't I read my new recipe for cheese biscuits all the way through before I started making them so I wouldn't have gotten to the end and read: "Sprinkle the remaining cheese on top"? (What remaining cheese?)

14. Why is it that the more I clean, the more I find things that need to be cleaned?

15. Why did two of my friends have to go and get hearing aids? Now they talk more softly (they used to be too loud), and now *I* can't hear!

And, finally,

16. Why is it, that whenever I'm having a bad day, I always feel better after having lunch with a girlfriend?

Now, that one I can answer.

Hello? Is Anyone Out There?

The other day I decided to change my hairdo. I had my hair cut, styled, and colored. I really liked my new look, so I went over to Sam's house to show him.

"Do you like it?" I asked, turning around slowly.

"What happened to your *old* hairdo?"

My *old* hairdo? The one you never said you liked?

I should have expected his reaction, though. Sam never tells me I look good. Once I did go out on a limb, on our way to a party, and asked him if he liked the dress I was wearing.

"I thought you were going to wear the green one," he said. "The one you look so good in."

Asking people for feedback – either about the way we look, or about our accomplishments – can be dangerous. The only kind of feedback we ever really want is the good kind. The kind that tells us we're wonderful.

Unfortunately, that's not always the kind we get.

A while back, during one of my annual job reviews, my boss praised my work. Then she added: "But I'd like to see more stress in your job."

Say what? I was already taking huge handfuls of vitamins and supplements to help me handle the stress. If my boss wanted me to have more stress, there was an easy solution. I could just stop taking them. Or, I could stop wearing make-up. Or, like in the commercial, I could change my hairspray. Maybe my hairspray was doing too good of a job. If I switched to a cheaper hairspray, maybe by the end of the day I would look more harried. Was that what she wanted?

Writers, especially, are people who need feedback. Positive comments motivate me to continue writing. I've found, though, that I need to be careful who I ask.

For example, I sent a copy of my first book to a girlfriend. She sent me a one-word email. "Cute."

When my mother saw my book for the first time, she told me she liked the cover. The cover was the only part of the book on which I'd had no input.

So, I'm going to go out on a limb and ask you for your feedback on how you like my writing, and how you think the book is going so far.

Here are four, short multiple-choice questions. Circle the statements you agree with.

1. Which of the following is true?

    a) I enjoy your stories so much, I read each one twice before I move on to the next one.

    b) My pet cat (dog/ hamster/ ferret) enjoys your stories so much that I read them aloud to him/her.

    c) I read your stories to my mother and even she laughs. (She also likes your cover.)

    d) I think you're right up there with John Grisham and Steven King. (Ha ha! I hope you think that's funny about comparing your writing to Steven King!)

2. I think your writing is:

    a) Hilarious! You have a great sense of humor!

    b) Witty and clever

    c) Motivational. It makes me want to be a better person.

    d) All of the above

3. I think your stories should be:

    a) Longer

    b) On the front page of the New York Times!

    c) Be made into a television series

    d) All of the above

4. Something I'd like to tell you:

   a) I think your publisher should give you a raise

   b) Reading your book is the best part of my day

   c) You saved my marriage! Reading your stories with my spouse has brought us closer together.

   d) All of the above.

And here's the essay question.

What has been your favorite chapter so far? (Be prepared to explain your answer with supporting details when we do the small group exercise.)

Thank you for taking this totally open and unbiased survey. Your answers are important to me. You could tweet them or text them to me if I had a cell phone that did either of those things.

My Trip to New York

In looking through a Road Scholar brochure the other day, I found a week-long program called "New York City at a Slower Pace." Since I was in the mood for an adventure, and the "at a slower pace" sounded about my speed, I signed up.

I was a little nervous about going to the Big Apple by myself. Any number of things could go wrong. I worried about:

How would I find my hotel?

How likely was it that I'd get lost?

Would anyone in the group like me?

Would I like any of them?

How much money should I take? What if I ran out of cash?

The reason cash was a concern was because on my return trip, I was going to be taking the airport limo from Indianapolis back to Lafayette. And when I made my reservation, the lady made it very clear that if I didn't have $27.00 -- CASH – the driver wouldn't let me on the bus.

But my biggest concern was: would I have a room to myself, or were they going to assign me a roommate? And if I got a roommate, would she be like the obnoxious woman who sat behind me on the last bus trip I took to Chicago who talked nonstop in a loud voice during the whole trip and gave me a headache?

At least one of my worries was relieved when I arrived at LaGuardia. There were plenty of signs directing me to where I could pick up my shuttle, and a lady at the welcome desk ordered the shuttle for me.

The directions I'd received from Road Scholar said that the airport was ten miles from the hotel, and that it would take about an hour and a half to get there. I was pretty sure that had to be a typo. Ten miles, in Indiana, is ten minutes. What were we going to be doing the rest of the time?

While I was waiting, I bought a one-dollar bottle of water for $3.86.

When the shuttle arrived, those of us who had been waiting crammed ourselves into the van. Luckily (well, not exactly luckily), the driver told me me sit up in front with him. Great! I'd have a front row seat. And there was plenty to see.

First of all, I got to see how rocky and pot-holed the roads were.

Secondly, I got to see how everyone in New York cuts in front of everyone else. Cars cut in front of us.

We cut in front of cars. We cut in front of big buses. We cut in front of cabs going two hundred miles an hour.

Our shuttle driver recklessly (at least it seemed to me) swerved in and out of traffic. It was like riding on the bumper car ride at a county fair. I kept my eyes closed for most of the trip. Whenever I opened them, I'd look out at the traffic in front of us, say "Holy shit!" to myself, then close my eyes again. I don't swear. I never swear. But I yelled "Holy shit!" for the ninety-minute trip into Manhattan.

I *did* have my eyes open to read the message on one of the overhead signs. It said: "This is U.N. week. Turn around and go home. The roads in New York City are all closed. We have enough traffic without you. Try again next week."

We tourists didn't know what U.N. week was, but we quickly learned "It's U.N. week" was the answer to many of our questions.

"Where's our bus?"

"Why can't I get a cab?"

"Why is there so much traffic?"

"Where do you suppose our guest-speaker is?"

New Yorkers didn't like U.N. week any better than we did. Cab drivers, bus drivers, and doormen just shook their heads while looking down the street at the blocked traffic.

Later that week, I learned that four million people commute into Manhattan every day. Four million! Is that even possible? I arrived on a Sunday. Does that go for Sunday, too?

The highlight of our death-defying ride from the airport to the hotel was when the driver turned right onto a very, very narrow street that had an SUV parked illegally on the right side of the street. The shuttle driver slowly started turning, but I could see the sweat on his brow. Could he make the turn without hitting the car?

Then he said to me: "Stick your head out your window and see if I'm going to make it."

Was he *kidding*? How would I know if he could make it? I didn't think we should even *be* on that road, let along turning a corner where we were obviously going to hit a parked car.

I rolled down the window, stuck my head out, and saw that there were about two inches between our shuttle and that car. Having already been in the shuttle for over an hour, and wanting badly to get to my room, I told him he had plenty of room. I closed my eyes and braced myself for the sound of metal crushing against metal. Somehow, he made it.

To get to Manhattan, we drove through a lot of old stuff. Old buildings. Old factories. Row houses with metal awnings and long sets of cement steps leading up to the front doors. Old electric lines. Old bridges. Old roads. Things that were crumbling. I felt like I was viewing ancient ruins in Rome. Why would anyone need to go to Rome when you can see such old stuff here?

Eventually we made it to Manhattan, and the driver began dropping everyone off at their hotels. Of course, mine was the last stop. But I had arrived.

My hotel, built in 1930, was quaint and adorable. There were six elevators on each side of the lobby. A security guard checked your room key to make sure you were supposed to be there. There were two restaurants off the sides of the lobby. One was formal – the other, less formal.

When I went to check in, I discovered that I'd won the lottery. Literally. There were three single women on the trip, and the people in charge of our program paired the other two women up and gave me a room to myself. I guess they actually did have a "drawing" to match who was going to room with whom.

I was thrilled to have a room of my own. It was on the 27th floor. To get there, I got off the elevator and turned left, and then left again, and then left again, and then left again. I was way off in a corner. It was a small, cozy room, that had large windows facing two directions. The view I liked best was looking out to the west where I could see the Hudson River.

Now, this is what I remember most about this trip: the view from my window. Have you ever seen the television series *Star Trek* --and there were several episodes where this happened -- where the crew on the spaceship looked out a window and saw something that was so unexpected that it freaked them out? Well, that's what the view was like for me.

Here at home, I live in a little cottage on a wooded lane. Looking out my front door, I can see my tiny front yard, a road (mostly gravel, that's only one-lane wide), and then a fence that surrounds my neighbor's house. I'm surrounded by trees. Because of the trees, I can't see a sunrise or a sunset. The trees are a blessing in the summer, but block the sun in the winter, so the ice on the lane never melts. I've lived in this house for 30 years and that's been my view.

In New York, I felt like I was on the spaceship Enterprise.

Parting my curtains, I could see a great expanse from the street down below to the top of the sky. I could see one hundred and eighty degrees from left to right. In the distance, I could see streets running all the way to the river. There were buildings of every shape and size. The newer buildings were rectangular, the older buildings were built up to a certain height, then the top levels were like stair steps going up to a peak.

At night I found myself just standing at my window and looking out. The colored lights from the streets and from the buildings looked like a humongous Christmas scene. It was so moving, I could almost imagine a baby in a manger down there on one of those streets even though it was still October.

Three things describe New York City: movement, noise, and energy. Along with Christmas, it was like the fourth of July. Walking down the street, there were street vendors, one of every kind of person, tattoo parlors, pawn shops, banks, restaurants, more restaurants, and even more restaurants.

As for sounds, there were sirens and jackhammers. But mostly you hear horns. Everybody honks in New York.

Back home, I think I heard one horn honk one time, and I'm sure the driver hit his horn by accident. We don't honk here. We're pretty laid back, and if we miss our light because the guy in front of us isn't paying attention, we give him the benefit of the doubt. He (or she) was probably doing something important so we're not going to get bent out of shape about it.

The larger buses honked at the smaller buses. The smaller buses honked at the cabs. The cabs honked at the cars. The trucks honked at the buses, the cabs, and the cars. Everyone honked at the pedestrians. When I first arrived in New York, there didn't seem to be any rhyme or reason to the honking. But after a few days I figured it out.

One beep meant: "MOVE!"

Two beeps meant: "You're an idiot!! MOVE!!"

Three beeps meant: "You're an idiot!! MOVE!!! You have two seconds, then I'm going to knock you from here to New Jersey."

The first night I thought I was going to have trouble adjusting to the nonstop energy there. But I got used to it. In fact, I had more trouble adjusting to coming back to the peace and quiet back home than I had being there.

During the week, we took in all of the regular touristy places: the observation deck at the Top of the Rock, Radio City Music Hall, St. Pat's cathedral (the 4th largest cathedral in the world!), the Statue of Liberty, Ellis Island, The High Line, a Broadway musical, and the Metropolitan Museum of Art.

All awesome.

Along with the interesting tours and great sites, there was good food and good weather. The twenty-four of us in the program hiked together, ate together, and told each other tall tales. We shared our favorite stories that we've told at home a million times, and that the people back home are tired of hearing.

None of us got robbed, although I did a pause for a moment when, at our opening session, our program coordinator told us if anyone on the street asked for our money, that we should give it to them. Say what? Give them my money? Should I try to explain to them that I need to keep $27.00 for my trip home?

There were no obnoxious people in the group. In fact, I got a little choked up when I said goodbye to everyone.

Luckily, I had managed to hold onto the $27.00 I needed for the bus trip home after I landed in Indianapolis. The ride from Indianapolis to Lafayette was much more subdued than the one from LaGuardia to Manhattan. Nobody cut in front of us. Nobody honked their horn. In fact, if you don't mind my saying so, it was downright boring.

Coming home was also a let-down. I unlocked my door, stepped inside, looked around, and thought: Who's going to make my dinner tonight? And, who's going to make my bed tomorrow?

I guess there's always a bit of a let-down when you come home after having a good time on a trip.

My cats *did* come out to tell me that they missed me. That helped. But the biggest help was in my mail.

A Road Scholar brochure. I sat down and started planning my next trip.

My Not-So-Much-Fun Book Reading Experience

I enjoy being asked to read from my books, and so far, I've only had positive experiences doing that. The only exception was the time when I read in the middle of the busiest restaurant in Indiana.

Knowing the restaurant's reputation, I expressed my concern about the possible noise level when the woman asked me to come and read to her group. The group had never been to that restaurant before, but the lady assured me that noise wouldn't be a problem. She'd reserved a private dining room off to the side of the main room.

When I arrived, I discovered that she was partially right. The small, private room *was* off to the side. There was one long table down the center of the room, and the ladies were crammed in shoulder-to-shoulder. Which wouldn't have been all that bad, except for the fact that the restaurant offered an "all-you-can-eat" buffet, so the ladies had to keep getting up to fill their plates.

The only door to our "private" room was an accordion door which had to remain open so people could go in and out to get their food. You had to walk through the main dining area to get to the buffet, and the restaurant was packed.

And it was noisy.

I wasn't due to read until after lunch, so at least my ladies wouldn't be getting up and down any more to get their food. As I was giving myself a pep talk that I could make this work, the waiter began seating people who weren't in our group at the six other tables in our room. And they were mostly men! I'd only planned to read to a woman's audience and was going to read my favorite pieces – including pieces about women's underwear, and sex.

I thought I should at least warn the men in the room about what was going to be happening, so I took a copy of my book around to them and introduced myself. I explained that we were going to be discussing women's undergarments and sex. One man said dryly: "We're familiar with those things." Looking back, he was probably working on divorce proceedings with his attorney.

The ladies finished eating and the woman in charge of the group signaled that it was time for me to read. The noise level was still high.

I began reading in a loud voice. The ladies at the far end of the long table couldn't hear me, so I began shouting. Was I going to be able to shout for 30 minutes? It wasn't the best way to appreciate my stories – I can't be very expressive when I'm shouting.

Then things got worse. The waiter came back in and started taking orders for coffee. Twenty ladies asked for 20 version of coffee.

"Do you have decaf?"

"Could I have half decaf and half regular?"

"Do you have non-dairy creamer?"

"Do you have Sweet'N low?"

"Could I get more water?"

"What kind of tea do you have?"

I tried to read even louder.

Then things got worse. After drinks were served, and I was practically hoarse, the waiter began distributing their checks.

"This isn't my check."

"I think that's MY check."

"Did you have soup and salad?"

"No, I had the buffet."

"Well, this must be your bill then."

I decided a change was in order. Maybe it would help if I moved to the other end of the room. While continuing to read, I moved to the opposite end of the crowded table, by the accordion door.

I thought that might focus people's attention on me. It didn't.

So, I decided to make the change I'd wanted to make from the beginning. While holding my scripts in my left hand and still reading and looking at my audience, I reached up with my right hand and began pulling the accordion door shut.

Unfortunately, I hadn't seen that there was a tray piled piled high with dirty dishes right there. When the accordion door hit the stand, down went all the dishes with a loud crash.

The waiter was very sweet. He told me he'd pick the dishes up.

That did it for me. I hurried and read my last piece, and the moment I finished, I exited as gracefully as I could.

I'm not sure anyone even noticed my departure.

They'd all decided to have dessert and were getting up to return to the buffet.

I Want You to Take the Centerpiece

Then there was the time I was invited to do a book reading for a very, very classy women's group in a very, very classy restaurant. The group consisted of university deans, department heads, and vice presidents, so the whole time I was conscious of trying to be on my best behavior.

We had a room to ourselves that was quiet. And the reading went well. The ladies laughed and seemed to enjoy my program.

It was getting out of there that was the problem.

Afterwards, I stayed and visited the appropriate length of time. Then I packed up my books and props to leave. The hostess of the event pointed to a large centerpiece of dried flowers that was on one of the tables. She told me she'd like me to have it.

Well, I can't have flowers in my house. My cats eat them – live or dried. So, I thanked her and told her I didn't need the centerpiece.

She told me she wanted me to have it.

I told her it was a beautiful centerpiece, but that I really couldn't use it.

She picked it up and repeated that she wanted me to have it.

I thanked her again and started to make my departure.

Again, she insisted that I take the centerpiece.

Now, I was a little out of my element. I figured that in this circumstance, it was important to be polite. I could take the centerpiece and give it to someone. Or take it and just throw it away. So, I agreed to take it. She followed me out to my car and put it on the floor of my front seat.

I thanked her and drove away.

I knew I couldn't take it into the house. The cats would eat it and then throw up all over everything.

I couldn't think of anyone to give it to.

I was too tired to drop it off at Goodwill.

I decided to go home and have dinner, then sit and put my feet up, and after that, go get it out of the car and take it to the trash.

Luckily, I forgot about it.

Until that evening, when I got the call.

"Sally? This is Esther from the woman's group you spoke to today. I'm embarrassed to ask you this, but could we have that centerpiece back? The granddaughter of one of our members made that for her grandmother, and it's very sentimental to their family. She had told us to make sure we got it back after the luncheon."

So, the next day I returned it.

To this day, I wonder what I would have told her if I had thrown it away . . .

Are There Green Vegetables in Kentucky?

After my mom passed, I used to have conversations with her in my head. Sometimes I even wrote her little notes, like the following that I wrote on a bus trip I recently took to Kentucky.

Dear Mom,

Good morning! Well, here I am, riding on a tour bus on my way to see some of the sights in the great state of Kentucky. We'll be on the bus for quite a few hours today, and I'm grateful that I packed my one pair of really baggy pants. The only thing is, I wish I'd worn them on the bus today because the pants I'm currently wearing are too tight.

P.S. And my feet are cold. I wish I'd worn my heavier socks (which are packed away in my suitcase along with the baggier pants.)

Dear Mom,

We have a woman tour guide on our bus! Her bus company calls their tour guides "escorts," not tour guides. I think "escort" means something else entirely, but that's just me, so I'm not going to say anything.

She's *very* professional. Except for what happened this morning. She was holding her cup of coffee, making the morning announcements from the front of the bus, when the driver had to make a quick stop.

She lost her balance, spilled her coffee, and landed in his lap. She assured us that that doesn't happen very often. The funny thing was, the bus driver didn't seem to mind having her in his lap.

Dear Mom,

I am SO thankful that the six busloads of school children that we saw when we pulled up for our riverboat cruise on the Ohio River were not on our boat.

Dear Mom,

For lunch today, there was a buffet on the riverboat and the main course was chicken. The little white plastic knife and the little white plastic fork they gave us (both of which bent when I was using them) made the meal quite interesting! At least I didn't break my knife off when sawing the chicken like some of the other people in our group did.

And luckily there was a large supply of napkins.

Dear Mom,

There was a band for our entertainment tonight. I could tell they were really trying, but if you'd been their mother, you would have sent them down to the basement to rehearse a few more times before they performed.

Dear Mom,

Let me tell you about this state-of-the-art bus! The seats recline almost to a prone position. In fact, the lady's head from the seat in front of me is currently in my lap, but that's O.K. It's only a six-hour trip, and her hair looks clean. She's smiling -- so I won't disturb her.

Dear Mom,

Remember how you used to pack us bologna sandwiches to take to school? That I understood. But – get this – at the last restaurant we stopped at they had "thick-sliced fried bologna" as their special of the day. Seriously? I had to laugh!

Dear Mom,

Well, I learned a valuable lesson today – that I should read descriptions of tours in brochures more carefully before I take a trip.

The description of today's trip said we'd be riding first class on a scenic railroad to look at the beautiful thorough-bred horses for which Kentucky is so well known.

When I read the words "first class," I expected the Orient Express. Unfortunately, what *they* meant by "first class" was that the passenger car we rode in, which was built in the 1950's, was, in *those* days, "first class."

They really got me on that one!

I also had trouble agreeing with their use of the term "scenic." They must have been referring to the trees along the tracks. I guess I should look at it this way. They were the same kind of trees we have back in Indiana. So, I felt right at home.

The bad news was: we only saw one horse! And it was way off in the distance.

I was all set to complain to the tour company about not seeing any horses, but before I did that, I decided to pull out the brochure and re-read the description of the train trip. It read:

"Enjoy the springtime scenery passing through horse farms en route to the palisades of the Kentucky River."

So, they only promised a horse *farm*. Not a horse! They sure got me on that one!

Dear Mom,

Do you remember how hard it was to get us kids to eat our vegetables? Sometimes you made us sit at the table until we finished them – and then they got cold! Well, you'd be proud of me. I now eat green vegetables. In fact, I LOVE green vegetables.

The problem is: On this particular trip, we had a large bus full of people, and to feed everyone in a hurry, we kept stopping at fast food places to eat. (Not my favorite thing to do.) And either they don't eat green vegetables in Kentucky, or the places where we stopped to eat had never heard of green vegetables.

After two days, I was desperate for a green vegetable. Any green vegetable. We were on our own for lunch, so I asked the curator at the museum we were at what the best restaurant in town was. He told me it was right down the street. So that's where I went.

Lo and behold, they had a whole list of green vegetables posted in magic marker on a sheet of paper on the wall. I began by asking for my favorite: okra.

The young girl who was our waitress took my order, went to the kitchen which was in the rear of the restaurant, then came back to the table and apologized. They didn't have okra.

O.K. I'll take peas. She took my order, then came back to the table and apologized again. They didn't have peas.

Same thing with brussels sprouts.

And green beans.

And turnip greens.

She was getting discouraged. Her feet were probably sore from making so many trips to the kitchen. So, I decided to change my approach. This time, I asked: "What green vegetables DO you have?"

"Oh!" She said, her face lighting up at the prospect of finally being able to please me.

"We have French fries!"

Dear Mom,

We have the neatest bus driver! He tells us jokes while he's driving and he doesn't get upset when we don't always come back to the bus when he tells us to.

When we come back late, he tries to make up for lost time and get us back on schedule. I heard him telling someone that his job would be a lot easier if police cars still had bubble lights on top, like they used to. The next time you talk to God, could you get him to put lights on top of police cars again so our driver can see them?

Like I said, he's a really neat guy!

Dear Mom,

Today we went to see the replica of Noah's Ark outside of Cincinnati. The size of the Ark was simply amazing. They said that a million visitors go through the Ark every year.

Unfortunately, all million were all there on Memorial Day while we were there.

Dear Mom,

Well, we're headed home -- almost back in Lafayette. I'm already thinking about where to go next year.

What do you think about Paris? Surely they have green vegetables in the restaurants there!

But, just to play it safe, maybe I should check it out.

What Should I Have Said?

Is it me, or are there times when people say things and you have no idea how to respond? Here are some things that have happened to me:

Situation #1:

A while back, I was asked to speak at a Book Lover's Club at a local retirement center.

Before I began my program, I sat and visited with the ladies, looking for things we had in common. Obviously, we had books in common, so I asked the logical question: "What book is your club currently reading?"

Everyone stared at me. Then, the hostess explained: "Oh, we don't *read* books. We just *love* them."

It was my turn to be caught off guard. Well, it must be working for them. The club's been in existence for a hundred years.

Situation #2:

This morning, when I got to the elementary school where I tutor, I decided to stop in the girl's room before I went to my classroom. There were four brand new kindergarteners at various stages of using the facilities – playing with the doors to the stalls (to see how far they would open), trying to get some soap out of the soap dispenser (like who can do that?), and trying to make the hand dryer stop blowing hot air (ain't gonna happen).

Outside, in the hallway, their teacher was calling for them to hurry up and join the rest of the class.

I decided to just stand there and stay out of their way.

A cute little blond went into a stall, then came out almost right away. She walked up to me, looked me straight in the eye, and reported loudly: "I tried, but I didn't have to go."

Then she waited for my response.

The first thing that came to mind was: "Do I know you?"

I also thought of saying: "Good to know."

I also thought of asking her to wait for a minute, and then I could tell her how the event went for me.

I ended up simply praising her for trying. She skipped off to class, and I was left to give myself my own praise.

Situation #3:

This morning I got on an elevator and pushed the button for the 5th floor. Just before the doors closed, a young mother pushing a baby carriage got on. The baby carriage was so large that it took some maneuvering to get it, and herself, onto the elevator.

Since I was standing in front of the panel of buttons, (and since I wanted to help her in some way), it made sense for me to push the button for the floor she was going to.

So, I asked her the logical question: "Where are you going?"

She answered: "Up."

I only thing I could think of saying was: "What kind of 'up'?" but it didn't come out. We just stared at each other.

What should I have said?

Situation #4:

This summer, I was asked to teach a writing course to a group of senior citizens at a retirement community. The only thing I knew about them was that they were in their 80's and 90's. I had no idea what kind of writing they wanted to do, what their writing abilities were, or at what level I should start the class.

So, I prepared a number of different activities, and lessons, at a number of different levels. When I'd meet them the first time, I'd get the answers to my questions.

Or so I thought. At the first lesson, I realized that I should probably start with the easiest activity I'd prepared. It was something rather clever (or so I thought), to just get them thinking about words and writing.

The activity was: What is your favorite letter of the alphabet? I explained that they could choose any letter they wanted. There was no right answer.

Then I shared that my favorite letter was "S." My two names, Sally and Sara, both start with the letter "S." And "S" is a powerful letter because it can make words plural.

After choosing their letter, they were to write down three words that started with that letter. The words I had chosen were "soon," "suppertime," and "solace."

I explained that I like the word "soon" because it leads me to believe that something nice is going to happen. My mother used to tell us that dinner would be ready "soon." So that word fills me with anticipation.

I chose the word "suppertime" because it's my cats' favorite word. I can be in any room of the house – at any time of day -- and say "suppertime," and the cats will race to the kitchen and jump up on the counter to be fed.

My third word was "solace." I explained that at night I sleep with a large stuffed animal – a mouse who wears a purple, gingham dress and nightcap – trimmed with white ruffles. I fall asleep holding her in my arms. She brings me great solace and comfort.

Now it was their turn.

First, what was their favorite letter? We went around the room. One gentleman chose "F." The next lady chose "M." The third lady could not commit to a letter, so the others in the group tried to help. She either didn't remember the alphabet, or she simply couldn't choose. So, the group decided to choose "R" for her, since her name was "Rosemary."

After everyone had committed to a letter, I asked them to write a list of words that started with that letter. I gave them five minutes to write the list in their brand-new notebooks. Most of the people just sat there (thinking?), but one lady began writing in earnest. She wrote. And wrote. And wrote. And wrote. Ah, now I knew who my star pupil was going to be! This was going to work out, after all.

When I asked for their responses, my student who had selected the letter "F" offered up the words "official" and "facial." "Official" didn't start with an "F," but since it contained TWO "f's, I gave him full credit.

I also commented on his selection of the word "facial" as opposed to "face." Of the two, I would have chosen the simpler word "face." I thought it was interesting that the word "facial" came to his mind instead of "face." Maybe this was going to be a neat activity because it was going to tell me things about them.

Rosemary, who had had difficulty choosing a favorite letter, had also not written down any words. The group helped her out by offering the word "rose."

Basically, it was like pulling teeth. But I had saved the best for last.

It was time to hear from my star pupil. The one who had written a list of words that started with "M" for the full five minutes. The one I was going to design the class around. The one who was going to make this a meaningful experience for the rest of the class, and for me.

"Fern, would you tell us your words?"

Fern sat back comfortably in her seat, adjusted her reading glasses, and began:

"When I was a little girl, I was at my grandmother's house, and my grandmother had to go down into the basement and it was a dark and scary place, and I accidently shut the door and the door got stuck and my grandmother was stuck in the basement."

I just sat there while she looked at me for my response.

What should I have said?

Situation #5:

I live in a darling, little cottage with a tiny little front yard. When you look out from my front door you see a lane, just wide enough for one car. And on the other side of the lane is a 10- foot fence. The fence surrounds a magnificent dwelling. I guess you could call it a small mansion.

My house looks like the woodcutter's cottage for that mansion. What I'm trying to explain is that the people who have lived in that house and I aren't exactly in the same socio-economic class. So, I've never met my neighbors.

But a few years ago, the mansion was sold. I kept an eye open to see who'd moved in, but never saw anyone coming or going. I was determined to say "hello" if I ever found any of them outside in their front yard.

The other day I did. I was on a walk, and as I passed the front of their house, I saw the mother and her two sons standing in their driveway. The mother was wearing a hat which blocked some of her face, but when I said "Hello," she smiled a friendly greeting.

So, I walked and introduced myself.

After I did that, she introduced herself. And then she introduced her twins.

I wouldn't have known they were twins if she hadn't told me. One was tall and had dark hair. The second one was short and blond. One was rather chubby, and the other one was quite skinny.

"This is my son Ralph," she said, putting her hands on the taller boy's shoulders.

"And this is my son John," she said, touching the shoulders of the second twin. Both boys smiled quietly and shook my hand.

Then, she corrected herself.

"No, *this* is my son Ralph," she said, pointing to the smaller blond. "And *this* is my son John."

Neither boy flinched or acted surprised.

While I was trying to relearn their names, she changed her mind again.

"No, THIS is my son Ralph, and THIS is my son John."

At which point I said I was happy to meet them and excused myself.

Was she confused? Was she in witness protection? Should you ask someone if they're in witness protection? What should I have said?

Twenty-eight Dollar Profit

I get tickled over the littlest things. The other day I delivered a couple of my books to a lady who had called me and asked to purchase them. As I left her house, I lovingly fingered the twenty- dollar bill, the five- dollar bill, and the three ones that were in my pocket.

"I'm rich!" I thought. "I'm wealthy!" "I have twenty-eight dollars that are mine. All mine!"

On my way home, I stopped to buy cat food. The bill was $28.00.

I either need to sell more books or get rid of the cats.

Something for Goodwill?

A couple of weeks ago Sam drove me up to my family reunion in northern Indiana. We left in plenty of time, so I talked him into stopping at the large mall in Merrillville.

Well, it happened to be a day when there were a lot of sales, so I "did" the mall while Sam patiently slept on the hard, wooden benches outside each store. I'd gotten some good bargains and we were on our way back to the car when I spotted Carson Pirie Scott. We don't have a Carson Pirie Scott store in Lafayette, so I deposited Sam on yet another bench and went in to see what I could find.

I found some wonderful bargains! When I went to check out, I noticed that the line was exceptionally long, but everyone seemed cheerful, and the salespeople seemed to be doing their best to keep the line moving.

When I got up to pay for my three items, the saleslady asked if I'd brought in something for Goodwill.

I had no idea what she was talking about. So, I told her, "no," that I was from out-of-town and had just stopped in for the day.

So, she rang me up, put my new things in a bag, and I left – quite happy.

On my way out, I heard two women talking. It turned out that if you brought in a donation for Goodwill, you'd get an extra 20% off your bill.

Darned! I could have done that! I could have stripped while I was there in line, handed the saleslady my clothes, and put on the new clothes – at 20% off!

Next time, I'll do that.

Daydreaming the Day Away

Daydreaming is one of my favorite pastimes. I think everyone should daydream on a regular basis. Here's why:

First of all, you can do it anywhere. *My* favorite place is during staff meetings.

Let's say I'm in a really boring staff meeting. What I try to do is look like I'm listening, but what I'm really doing is playing the song "Now I've . . . had . . . the time of my life" in my head while dancing with Patrick Swayze.

When I reach the apex of boredom, I picture myself running across the dance floor and into Patrick's outstretched arms whereupon he lifts me up over his head like he did with Jennifer Grey in *Dirty Dancing*.

The one thing I have to be careful of is not to have too big of a smile on my face or else my boss will call on me for my opinion of which I have none since I haven't been paying attention.

The second reason I enjoy daydreaming is because I can go wherever I want. I especially enjoy going back in time and reliving some of my favorite memories. Like Thanksgivings at my Grandad

Coffman's farm. My grandparents didn't live on their farm (they lived in town), but they bought a farm with a barn for horses and an apple orchard for apples, and that's where our family gathered to celebrate holidays.

There was an old farmhouse on the property, and as soon as we arrived, my Grandad would go down to the cellar and start a fire in the coal furnace. It took a long time for the house to get warm. We kids weren't used to a cold house, so we'd huddle together over the big vent in the kitchen floor to soak up the heat while the house was warming up.

And the food! There was a long table that stretched out from one end of the kitchen to the other. Everybody brought food. One year, my mother counted and discovered there were as many pies as there were people – we could each have our own pie.

After the meal, we kids spent the day playing in the bales of hay in the barn. Not only were we allowed to get dirty, but it was the one day out of the year that we didn't get yelled at for doing things we shouldn't have been doing. The adults were in the house too busy visiting to watch what we were doing.

The third reason I enjoy daydreaming is because I can do things in my head that I can't do in real life.

For instance, I've invented this really cool movement where I have the ability to dance on my toes like a ballerina, and then, when I want to, I can put my foot down and slide it across the floor (or the ground) like I'm ice skating. I'm thinking about how I might patent it. People could switch from dancing to ice skating without having to change their shoes.

The final thing I like about daydreaming is that I can be with all sorts of neat people.

For instance, Yul Brynner. In my head, Yul Brynner sees me across the room, comes over, and asks me to dance the "Shall We Dance" number from *The King and I*. It takes forever for us to get through the dance because on the first turn, discovering that I'm in his arms, I collapse in ecstasy and he has to catch me and hold me up and then we both laugh, and laugh, and laugh.

Eventually, we finish the dance – in complete and utter joy.

Those are the reasons I like to daydream.

Please don't tell my boss.

If you promise not to tell my boss, I'll tell you my dreams about Willie Nelson.

That Won't be Enough

My favorite part of the exercise class I'm taking is at the end when the instructor has us relax for five minutes. She puts on soothing flute music, turns off the lights, and tells us to get comfortable in our chairs. She leads us through some deep breathing exercises where we raise our arms slowly above our heads while concentrating on a happy word for the day, such as "joy."

This morning, as we were lowering our arms and breathing out, she said: "When you blow out, blow all the negativity out of your system."

A voice from the back of the room whispered: "That's going to take more than one breath."

My Madras Bathing Suit

Proms were a really big thing at our high school. I went to my senior prom with a really, really, really neat guy. But what I remember most vividly was the fiasco with my bathing suit.

Our prom was a two-day affair. We'd go out to a restaurant for dinner, then drive to a large hotel in downtown Cleveland for the prom, then have an after-prom party back in our gym. Around 2 a.m., our parents would show up to serve us breakfast. We'd go home for a few hours' sleep, then drive to a lake and spend the day at the beach. It was truly an event.

Obviously, a new bathing suit was in order. My mom had set aside some of the household money for my prom dress, a trip to Chicago to buy my dress, getting my high-heel shoes dyed to the exact color of my dress (which took several trips to the shoe repair), a new pair of white gloves, a boutonniere for my date and, of course, money to get my hair done.

It wasn't easy, but I managed to also finagle her out of some money for a new bathing suit.

And I found the perfect suit! It was a two-piece. (Not a bikini.) The bottom was made of a stretchy jeans material, and the top was made out of a multi-colored blue madras print. It was awesome!

When I brought it home from the store, my mother approved. Until she read the tag which said: "Dry Clean Only." Dry clean only?? Who would make a bathing suit that was dry clean only?? Who would *buy* a suit that was dry clean only?

My mother insisted that I return the suit, but I explained that I wasn't planning on getting in the water. My hair would still be done up from the night before, and I wasn't about to get it wet. My plan was to lie on the beach all day and just look beautiful.

For days we argued about my returning the suit, but eventually I wore her down. And kept the suit.

But my mother had the last laugh.

For a while, my girlfriends and I did, indeed, look stunning lying there on our beach towels on the beach. But at one point our dates thought it would be fun to bring water up from the lake and soak us. From head to foot.

It took about two weeks before the stains from the dye in the madras came out of my skin.

Thought I Could Fit in

I thought when I got older that I'd stop doing dumb things. That hasn't been the case. I still do dumb things. One of the more common ways I get myself in trouble is when I try to be something I'm not.

My latest example is when I tried to fit in to a group of people much younger than I was. I would have been fine if I'd just acted my age. But for some reason, I wanted people to think I was younger than I really am.

Here's the story:

While looking for something to do, I came across an ad for a Ballroom Dance Club at a local university. I'd always wanted to learn to ballroom dance, so I went to my computer and clicked on their website.

According to the website, everyone was welcome to join – undergraduates, graduate students, faculty, staff, and people in the community. So, there would be people my age.

But somehow I got it in my head that I didn't want to stick out as an older person. So, when I went to their callout the next evening, I dressed as youthfully and college-y as I could – jeans and a university t-shirt.

And when I got there, I was going to act young and cool.

The test would be how I was treated when I walked into the ballrooms, where the callout was being held. As I approached the dancers handing out fliers at the door, I held my breath. Would they exchange glances at each other or roll their eyes when they saw me coming?

No. They greeted me as warmly as they did everyone else entering the room.

So, I'd done it! I'd fooled everybody! I fit in!

I took a seat and began chatting with the young undergraduate next to me. She didn't seem alarmed at my being there either. She probably thought I was a student, too. Again: confirmation that I fit in.

The room filled up quickly. I'm guessing there were about 200 people.

For about an hour, various members of the club demonstrated the kinds of dancing they'd be teaching in the classes. Between the demonstrations, the club president welcomed us and explained what we could expect should we decide to join. He explained that we'd need leather-soled shoes. He explained where and when the classes were going to be held. And he explained the club dues.

At the end of the hour, he said he'd like to have feedback on how the evening went. He asked everyone to please take out their cell phones, type in a specific website, and take a short survey.

Now this is where my disguise was blown.

One-hundred and ninety-nine students reached over, pulled their cell phones out of their backpacks, and hunched over and began taking the survey.

I don't have a cell phone.

I have a flip phone. But it was in my car. And it doesn't have internet access.

I thought about raising my hand and asking if they had a paper copy of the survey that I could take but decided not to do that.

I was the only person in the room sitting upright in a chair. Everyone else was hunched over, typing into their cell phones. I wanted to hunch over, too, so I bent over and retied my shoes.

At that point, I realized that this probably wasn't going to be the right club for me to join. Given my stamina and the state of my knees, I was pretty sure I wouldn't have been able to keep up with the class.

And, of course, there was that other little problem.

I didn't have the right kind of cell phone.

Ode to Lora

My college friend Lora Bell was one of the oldest souls I ever met. She was also one of the first people from whom I felt unconditional love. I read the following at her memorial service.

Ode to Lora

I met her in 1966
In COM 114, to be exact,
In those days, alphabetically, we sat.
Miss Bell on the right
Miss Coffman on the left.

We gave speeches
With passion and vigor
Befitting our intellect.

She spoke of the problems of organized religion
Compared, analyzed, professed, and the like.
I spoke of how to save leftovers in baggies.

And we became friends.
Miss Bell on the right.
Miss Coffman on the left.

She worked at an answering service
Knew everyone's number in town
The phone – even then – was her trademark.

We once drove to Cleveland to visit my family
Miss Bell on the right
Miss Coffman on the left.
She was enjoying her visit,
Then the clock struck 8:00
And my family and I went to bed
Leaving her – in the quiet house – wondering what to do.

For 32 years she reminded me of that evening.
Miss Bell on the couch
Miss Coffman in bed.

She went off to grad school
And became a teacher.
Oh, what a teacher
Extraordinaire.

She taught, as she wrote
From the heart.

We each married, divorced, had cats, wrote plays.
While she was professing, comparing, analyzing, and the
like.
I was finding new ways to use baggies.

Greeting cards were next
That made people laugh.
By phone we'd visit
Always longer on her bill than on mine.

She was so proud of her friends' achievements
And those of her sisters

And nieces and nephews.

She read higher level books than I
Kept hoping that someday I'd understand Toni Morrison
Saw higher level movies than I
Always probing, searching, analyzing, comparing and the like.
Viewed politics differently than I
Miss Bell on the left
Miss Coffman on the right.

Was always on a higher spiritual plane
Always patient with me and encouraging
The gentlest soul I have ever known
Looking now into the face of God
Probing, analyzing, and questioning
Getting to know everything she can about her new-found friend.

I'm blessed,
For 32 years I knew this bright, sensitive, creative creature
And was privy to her unconditional love.

And I thank God for COM 114
With Miss Bell on the right
Miss Coffman on the left.

It's Not That I'm Short. I'm Just Not Particularly Tall

I've never thought of myself as short. I have noticed, however, that when I look at myself in photographs, I don't go up as high up on the page as the people standing next to me do.

If I *were* short, though, I'd be all right with that. There are lots of advantages to being short.

For one thing, no one's intimidated by a short person. We're not a threat. We might bite you in the leg, but we're not intimidating.

Second, whereas tall people can't look shorter, short people *can* look taller. We can stand on a box. We can wear a hat. Or platform shoes. Or, do what I did back in high school – wear three-inch heels and tease my hair up into a beehive on top of my head.

I'll admit, there *are* some situations when my lack of height presents a problem:

1. When I'm on an airplane and try to put my suitcase in the overhead bin.

2. When I do a presentation for a group and the podium they've given me is so high that the audiences only see me from my nose up, and

135

3. When I'm in my "Ballet for Seniors" class and the teacher has us do glissades across the floor.

Those first two situations are pretty easily remedied. On a plane, I stand there and try to look as weak as possible until someone comes along and helps me. And when I schedule a presentation, I ask if they can provide a music stand (which can be raised and lowered) rather than a podium.

The glissades are another story.

I'm not sure what possessed me to take a "Ballet for Seniors" class in the first place. For most of the class, my fellow ballerinas and I stood in three rows facing the instructor and the mirrors. I always hid in the back row. But sometimes, near the end of the class, the instructor had us gather at one end of the room and do glissades across the floor, alone, to the other end.

How do you do a glissade? Let's say you're at the right side of the room, traveling to the left. You begin by raising your left knee to the side as high as possible. Then you kick it out, while at the same time jumping up as high as you can into the air. You then land on your leg (with your knee still bent) and bring your right leg in to touch your left foot.

Once your feet are together, you jump again. Over and over until you get to the other end of the room.

My fellow ballerinas, who'd all been taking this class for years, danced one-by-one, like graceful gazelles, across the floor.

The first time I tried it – well, every time I tried it -- *I* looked like a frog. Even when I jumped as fast as I could, I only managed to get about halfway across the floor by the time everyone else had reached the far end of the room. It took them an average of about 10 steps to cross the floor. It took me about 25. Then, the moment I finished my last glissade– doubled over and wheezing for air -- the instructor had us start back the other way.

Wait! They'd had a chance to rest! Where was *my* chance to rest?

I suffered through two more classes, then at the end of the third class, when it was time for the glissades, I ducked out and hid in the ladies' room.

Not long after that, I found a much gentler exercise class that was a lot more my speed. The fastest we go is walking in a big circle around the outside of the room.

So, that's my experience in dance class with having short legs.

Having short *arms* is a whole other issue. To get to my new exercise class, I have to park in a parking garage. And to exit the garage, I have to roll down my window and tap my parking pass up against a sensor.

Because my arms are so short, I have to pull up really close to the sensor. Everybody in line behind me takes bets to see if I run into the sensor, scrape the side of my car against it, or knock the entire side of the parking garage down.

In my next life, I'm going to ask to be a little taller.

Stories about Getting Older

Story #1: My Birthday

I just had one of the best birthdays I've ever had.

It began when I woke up – hungry -- at 4:00 a.m. I got out of bed, went downstairs, and made myself my favorite breakfast -- bacon, hashed browns, and eggs a la Sally. Eggs a la Sally are a lot like eggs over easy, but I'm not able to flip eggs without breaking the yoke, so I cook them on just one side, and when I go to put them on my plate, I flip them over so they look like eggs over easy.

Then I went back to bed.

At noon, my good friend Rosie bought me lunch at my favorite cafe. I had an Italian sausage and green pepper pizza with a gluten-free crust that was baked in a special brick oven.

That evening, my friend Rhonda made me dinner at her house. A T-bone steak, sweet potato with lots of butter, fresh asparagus, and a green salad. I topped it off with a big piece of dark chocolate.

Like I said, it was one of my best birthdays ever.

It was all about food.

When you reach a certain age, it's all about food.

Story #2: It's Also All about Perspective

I was going to be doing a reading from my books and had invited two friends – Rod and Sam -- who were both really good readers to read with me.

I needed to get Rod his scripts, so I took them to his office. I could barely understand him. He explained that his tongue was swollen. But he said he was on medicine for that and assured me he'd be O.K. by the time we did our reading the following week.

Meanwhile, Sam came down with shingles.

Then, since it was allergy season, my sinuses decided to clog up.

The day before the reading, I emailed Rod and asked him if his tongue was still swollen.

He answered: "Tongue is better and I should be able to read (or at least as good as I ever could)."

I wrote back: "Sam has shingles, I can't breathe through my nose, and you can't talk. We're going to be quite a three-some tomorrow."

Rod wrote back: "Wow. Will you and Sam feel like doing it or should we cancel?"

I responded: "We're both fine. At our age (Rod's a lot younger than Sam and me), shingles and allergies are a step up from how we usually feel."

Story #3: Losing my Car Keys

We all do this. We get ready to leave the house and can't find our keys.

That's what happened to me this morning. I had my coat on, slung my purse over my left shoulder, and went to pick up my keys, which I always leave on the kitchen counter next to the back door.

No keys.

I have a rule to *always* leave my keys on the counter so I can find them.

No keys. I must have broken my rule.

Went to the next most logical place I might have laid them. The dining room table.

No keys.

Checked my purse.

No keys.

I stopped to think. I reminded myself that I never break my rule, so they must be on the counter by my back door.

I went back to the counter by my back door.

No keys.

I went back to the next most logical place I might have laid them. The dining room table.

No keys.

I poured everything out of my purse onto the dining room table.

No keys.

I decided to try the *illogical* places I might have laid them. Where, in the house, had I been recently?

I walked through the dining room. The living room. The bathroom. The kitchen.

No keys.

I circled around a second time.

No keys.

I happened to look down at my left hand.

They were in my left hand.

Story #4: Losing my car keys *again*

Now that the weather's turned colder, I go out and start my car in the morning and let the defroster melt the ice off my windshield. The other day, that's what I did. I started the car, then went back inside to do the dishes while the car was warming up.

When it was time to leave, I carried a huge armload of books (that I was returning to the library) to the car and threw them onto the backseat. They fell out of my hands and scattered all over the seat.

I heard a clink (a sound the books couldn't have made), so I realized I must have dropped my car keys onto the seat. So I stood there in the cold and searched through the scattered books to try to find my car keys.

I couldn't find them.

They had to be there somewhere. I knew they were there somewhere.

No keys.

Where were the keys?

Then I remembered. The keys were in the ignition.

AARGH!

Story #5: Not keeping up with technology

Back in my day when I wanted to watch a movie, I'd get a VHS tape from the local library. VHS tapes were easy to use and easy to get out of their cardboard boxes.

Then DVDs came out. The other day, I checked one out of the library, returned home, and prepared to sit down and enjoy the movie. But I could NOT get the plastic container open. I tried everything. It would NOT open. It was obviously defective.

Wanting to test my theory of its defectiveness (before I went to the basement and used my hammer), I decided to go in search of a younger person to see if he (or she) could open it for me.

It was a beautiful, sunny day, so I went out my little lane to the street to look for someone to help me. I stood there for a long time, figuring that eventually someone would come along. And he did. Riding a bike.

I waved to him like I was hailing a taxi and he biked over to where I stood on the sidewalk. I showed him my defective DVD that wouldn't open.

He pushed on a little button (like where did he find THAT?) and the box flew open.

I now know how to open a DVD.

Was I embarrassed? Hell, no.

The only thing I regret was not finding out where he lived.

Ode to My Dad on His 81st Birthday

Dear Dad:
You still play golf in the rain.
It doesn't seem to have hurt your brain.

Bridge and rummy you still play,
Through the night and through the day.

You still bid 7 No Trump,
Although in mom's throat it does leave a lump.

You still give us advice
(whether we want it or not)
We don't always take it,
But it *does* hit the spot.

Your body's not getting old,
It's just getting better
Although it depends a lot on the weather.

So we're honoring you this day,
And saying "Hooray!"

Father always knows best.
So go take your rest.

A nap every day,
Will bring 82 years your way.

Ode to My Dad on His 83rd Birthday

Dear Dad:

This is the year you turn 83,
That's old for a horse, or even a tree!

It sounds a bit like a retired old train,
"Old 83" who stayed out in the rain.

But people still come to see "Old 83"
'Cuz he is as neat as a father could be.

Now, when your bones get to creaking and squeaking,
Be grateful your brain isn't beeping or leaking.

So, eat all these peanuts,
You don't need to share,

Just wanted you to know,
"Old 53" cares.

Message from My Dad

I had my dad for another ten years from the time I wrote that last poem. He was the love of my life, but in my family, we didn't outwardly display those kinds of emotions, or even talk about them. After he passed, there was so much that I wanted to tell him. I especially wanted to thank him for all the things he taught me.

At the same time I was grieving his passing, I was also struggling with a person in my life who was bullying me. It was someone I couldn't disengage from – I needed to interact with her on a regular basis. This had been going on for a long time. I didn't know how to deal with the situation, and it was starting to get to me.

One night, I went to bed with both my dad and the bully on my mind. And I had a dream. It was one of those dreams that was so real that when I awakened, I was convinced I'd been in another place and time.

They say you should write your dreams down so you'll remember them. Towards that end, I keep a pen and a pad of paper next to my bed. That night, I dreamed that my dad came and spoke the following words to me which I found the next morning written on the pad of paper.

I loved being your father. You were so full of life and joy and energy around me. You kept my spirit alive!

It's been a two-way street. Don't think you only learned from me. I also learned so much from you – you and your free spirit have been such a positive example for me and helped me to evolve to who I was in my later years.   I love you!

We don't just have wings on the other side. You have wings there, too, on earth.

Honor and use them. Keep your free spirit. Don't let anyone or anything dampen them!

They say that dreams can convey messages that help us cope, solve our problems, or give us reassurance. Although I don't remember doing it, I must have awakened during the night and written those words down. That dream brought me great comfort. It reassured me that not only did my dad know he'd been important to me, but that I'd been important to him, too.

I got great comfort from the second part of the message as well. My dad had once met the person who had been bullying me and had known the situation before he passed. When he said: "Don't let anyone or anything dampen your spirit" I think he was suggesting that I rise above the bully instead of continuing to do battle with her. I could use my "wings" to free myself from the situation.

And from that day on, I was no longer affected by that bully.

How I Got My Name

I need your help in trying to locate someone.

I'm trying to find the woman who, more than practically anyone else in the world, had the greatest impact on my life. This event took place on October 11ᵗʰ of 1948 in the maternity ward at the hospital in Bedford, Ohio.

I had just been born the previous day.

This lady came into my life for probably less than 30 minutes and my family (and I) never saw her again. She was filling in for the regular social worker whose job it was to help mothers fill out their baby's birth certificates.

This lady, let's call her SSW (for Substitute Social Worker) pulled up a chair next to my mother's bed, licked the tip of her pencil to prepare to write, and hunched over her clipboard.

"What name have you chosen for your baby?" she asked.

Now, in those days, it was a common practice to put women to sleep when they were giving birth, so when SSW met my mom, my mom was still pretty groggy. My dad was at work.

My parents had decided to name me "Sally." I'm not sure how they picked that name. But it was determined that I was going to be "Sally."

So, my mother said: "Sally."

And this lady – this SUBSTITUTE social worker – told my mother that "Sally" wasn't a proper name. I couldn't be named "Sally."

So, my mother in her state of grogginess, explained that to my dad when he came to visit that night, and my parents, believing her, went back to the drawing board.

The closest thing they could come up with was "Sara Jane." There had been a "Sara Jane" in our family, way back when. So, my birth certificate says I'm "Sara Jane," but my folks have always called me "Sally."

Now you may not think that's so awful, but FOR MY ENTIRE LIFE, I'VE HAD TO EXPLAIN TO PEOPLE WHAT MY NAME IS! I've spent thousands of hours explaining why I go by "Sally" when my name is really "Sara Jane."

Having two names is a problem every time I have to sign in somewhere, like at a doctor's office. Invariably when they ask my name, I give them the wrong one.

"Sally Coffman" I'll say.

They check their computer. "We don't have a Sally Coffman. Are you SARA Coffman?"

Or, the reverse.

"Sara Jane Coffman" I'll say.

"We don't have a 'Sara Jane.' Are you 'Sally'?"

Aargh!

I'll admit, there was a time that having two names almost worked to my advantage. I was scheduled to do a book reading at a retirement home, and during the planning stages, I was in contact with two of their activities' coordinators, neither of whom I had met. All of the arrangements were made by phone.

They must not have coordinated their efforts, because they thought I was two different people.

When I showed up for the reading, they each handed me a check: one filled out to "Sara Jane Coffman," and the other filled out to "Sally."

After explaining that I was just one person, I handed them back one of the checks.

The thing is: parents today name their daughters all sorts of things! I wonder what SSW would think of:

Summer, Halo, Candle,

Africa, Amethyst, Peony,

Zoe, Echo, Keeli,

Storm, Skye, Easter,

Sami, Heaven, or Charlie,

Parents are even giving their daughters the names of states, like Arizona, Texas, Indiana, Florida, Missouri, Tennessee, and Carolina.

And even when parents use old-fashioned names, they sometimes spell them in unusual ways, like: Kathe, Jayne, Baylee, or Caren.

If I find that SSW, I'm not going to be upset with her. But there's a site on the internet called: "Baby Names Guaranteed to Shock Grandma." If I find her, I'd like to show her that site and let her read through some of those names . . . just so I can see the expression on her face.

I'll admit, there is one advantage to having two names. When someone calls me on the phone and asks for "Sara Jane," I know to hang up. They're either asking for money or trying to sell me something.

To My Dear Friend A.J.

The loss of a friend is always difficult. This letter is a tribute and a memorial to my dear friend A.J.

Dear A.J.,

I'm writing this letter to tell you what a profound influence you had in my life – personally, professionally, and spiritually.

Let's start with spiritually. Do you remember the time when I stopped by to chat, and you were reading a book about The Twilight Zone? I knew that had been a TV show back in the '60's, but I'd never watched it. You suggested I read the book. I did. It motivated me to check some of the old shows out of the library to watch. I was fascinated by them.

They opened my eyes that there could be another world out there. And that someday -- in a flash of a second -- I might come face-to-face with that other world. And most importantly, that when I do, I'm going to be O.K. Those thoughts are both incredibly exciting and incredibly reassuring to me.

Second, I'll never forget the play *Never Too Late* that you directed where you cast me in the role of the daughter. What an experience that was! I saw Daisy (the woman who played the mother, who'd never been in a show before) at church the other day. We hugged each other, as we always do when we meet, with great fondness. And the gal who helped me change costumes for that show became, and is, my best friend. We have lunch together almost every week.

Third, I'm learned so much from you when we played husband and wife in *Guilty Conscience* together. Here's what I remember: for all 12 performances, you came out onstage with a different persona -- which truly kept me on my toes. Every moment of the show stayed fresh for me. Your character was a manipulative son-of-a-gun, and no one could have captured that manipulation like you did.

In other plays I've been in, I always worried about remembering my lines. I never worried about my lines when I was onstage with you. You connected (and captivated me) to such an extent, all I had to be is near you and the words came out.

Fourth, I loved the cruise that you and your wife and Sam and I took to the Caribbean. I especially remember the night the four of us were out on the front of the ship goofing off and taking pictures, pretending that we were filming the movie *Titanic*. A huge wind storm came up, and it's a wonder that we didn't all get swept overboard. As I recall, no one on the ship knew we were out on deck, and minutes after we fought through the wind to get back inside, the doors were locked so no one could go out there.

You were as great a comedy reader as you were an actor. Do you remember the time when we finished doing our program for an audience and the person in charge asked us to stay so the audience could ask us questions? We all sat down, but one of the readers had already put your chair away, so when you went to sit down, you went all the way to the floor. You fell with such grace! And the funny faces you made as you got back up got the biggest laugh of the day.

And, finally, I have fond memories of reading *Love Letters* with you up at Pokagon State Park. Our director's wife told me that her husband thought the show was "pretty good." A real compliment since she said her husband never thinks anything is good. So, we must have done something right.

I'm so grateful that our lives crossed. I know that with your gift for teaching and passion for learning that you're busy teaching and taking classes, and helping others grow and learn. And I know you're as loved by everyone "up there" as much as you were "down here."

With great love and affection, and until we meet again,

Sally

I Didn't Go to The Prom That Year

Proms were a really big deal in my neighborhood when I was growing up. Everyone on our street celebrated prom night almost as much as we did Halloween.

I lived on a street with identical cookie-cutter houses all in a line on both sides of the street. Word spread quickly if one of the girls on our block was going to the prom.

Families would come out and sit on their porches to watch the arrival of the young man coming to pick up his date. He'd be wearing a white tux and black bow tie. His car (or his dad's car) would be polished like it had never been before.

We'd watch him carry a box with his date's corsage to the front door. He'd be invited in for pictures. Then, there would be picture-taking out on the front steps. By this time, the two prom-goers would be anxious to get away, so the young man would walk her carefully to his car. If you were close enough, when he opened the car door, you could see the white sheet that he had carefully laid on top of the floor mats so the hem of her dress wouldn't get dirty.

Sometimes the neighbors would exchange glances to each other, and you could tell they were remembering their first dates, or their first proms. After seeing the couple off, we'd all go back inside and continue watching *Lawrence Welk*, or the *Mickey Mouse Club*, or whatever else might have been on at the time.

I was lucky enough to have been invited to the senior prom when I was just a sophomore. That was a big deal! My mother took me to a dressmaker who made me a beautiful long gown out of pink satin. I had several fittings and felt like a fairy princess every time the dressmaker fussed over fitting the dress to me. I loved the dress, but my mother liked it even better because it had straps. (The style of the day was strapless.)

I wore high-heeled shoes dyed to match my dress and long, white gloves. And, I had my hair done up on my head as high as possible, since my date was about a foot taller than I was.

Everyone in the neighborhood watched that year as I was the one getting my picture taken and being walked to my date's car. And I had a wonderful time at the prom.

So, the next year, when I was a junior, I knew from the first day of school that I wanted to go to the prom.

I picked out the senior that I wanted to have ask me and started flirting with him whenever I could. He flirted back, but never asked me out. That was O.K. Just as long as he asked me to the prom.

Starting in January, the guys began asking gals to go to the prom with them. No invitation yet for me.

I continued flirting.

February came. At least half of the girls in the senior class had dates for the prom.

I continued flirting.

March came. Almost everyone had a date for the prom. This was not looking good. More than ever, I was determined to go to the prom. I came to the decision that I was going to go, even if I couldn't go with Mr. Wonderful.

So, I began looking around. With just three weeks left, I decided to accept an invitation from anyone who asked.

And someone did. A shy senior guy who I talked to every day (we were both hall guards during third period) asked me if I'd like to go to the prom with him. We'd never gone out together, but he was a sweet, quiet guy. Finally. A date to the prom!

So, I said "yes."

I ran home that night, told my folks, and began making plans. Where could I get a dress? What color should it be? Would there be time to dye my shoes? Make a hair appointment?

Then, the next day, the fantasy I'd had all year came true. Mr. Wonderful came up to me while I was standing at my locker before school and asked me if I'd go with him to the prom.

Mr. Wonderful! Mr. Wonderful! Fireworks went off! I could go to the prom with Mr. Wonderful!

But what about Shy Guy? I didn't want to hurt his feelings, but I was pretty sure he'd understand if I broke my date with him. After all, he and I had never gone out together, and we'd only had the date for the prom for less than a day.

So, that morning, during our time in the hall together, I explained the situation to Shy Guy. Knowing I'd had a crush on Mr. Wonderful all year, he told me to accept his invitation and go and have a good time. He said: "no problem." He'd ask someone else.

Perfect!

At the end of the day, I found Mr. Wonderful and accepted his invitation. Miracles did happen! Not only was I going to the prom, but I was going with the guy I'd had a crush on all year!

That night at dinner, I told my folks about the change in plans.

To say that they were appalled would be an understatement. Not only were they appalled, they told me I wasn't going to go to the prom with anyone.

"You don't change plans just because you get a better offer."

What? Who says? Why not? Couldn't I? Just this once?

I explained that Shy Guy was O.K. with my breaking our date. That he was going to ask someone else.

That didn't matter. "You don't change plans just because you get a better offer."

In the next few days, everyone at school heard about what had happened. My friends' parents called my parents to congratulate them for their decision to not let me change dates like that.

And, so, that year, I stood on my front porch with everyone else in the neighborhood and watched the senior boys pick up their dates. Then went back inside to watch *The Lawrence Welk show*, or the *Mickey Mouse Club,* or whatever else might have been on at the time.

As hard as it was to learn: "You don't change plans just because you get a better offer" has stuck with me -- and served me well -- throughout my life.

Moments I'd Like to Do Over Again

Do you ever wish you could go back and do some of the things in your life over? I don't mean going back and correcting your mistakes (like being able to go to that prom I missed). I mean, actually re-living your very happiest moments. I have four such moments that I'd do over.

The first one involves the famous actress Helen Hayes. In the film *Airport* she played the little old lady stowaway. She stole the show with her million ways to sneak past security and ride for free on airplanes.

I had the great good fortune of seeing her on Broadway.

When I was in college, my parents lived in New Jersey. My mom and I had free passes to take the train into New York City, so the two of us would go into New York to see Broadway plays.

When we went to see Helen Hayes, we had great seats -- front row center. Helen Hayes was playing an older "mother" character. In the scene that I remember, she was rocking in a rocking chair, close to the front of the stage, directly in front of me. She was having a boisterous fight with her son and there was a box of chocolates (that he'd given her) on her lap.

At one point in the fight – when it got really heated – she jumped out of the rocking chair, and the chocolates flew all over the stage.

I was so engrossed that I stood up and reached out to start to help her pick up the chocolates.

I'm sure she had to notice me standing up and reaching out. I wonder what she thought. Did she realize the connection she'd made with me? Did she realize that she made me feel like I was actually there in that kitchen with her?

I'd love to relive that moment with her again.

Another time I was that involved in an event was when I helped my friend Tina go through labor and delivery.

Tina had asked me to drive her to the hospital when it was time to go, and she called me the night she started having contractions. As it turned out, we had to drive through an intense snowstorm to get to the hospital. Although it was bitterly cold outside, I sweated profusely, worrying that I wouldn't get her there on time.

The doctor arrived by snowmobile.

It turned out to be the most magical night of my life. After the baby was born, the doctor handed him to me and let me give him a bath in a bowl of warm water.

I felt like I was holding a piece of God.

I'd love to give Christopher his bath all over again.

On the other end of the life cycle is our passing from this world to the next. And I was privileged to be with my dad during his last few days on earth.

He was in hospice. My brother and sister and I were taking turns staying in his room with him.

One afternoon, my dad partially sat up in bed and started talking to someone directly in front of him. And he was mad! You could see on his face that he was upset with the person he was talking to. He was frowning, and shaking his head "no." That went on for a long time. First, he'd talk, then the other person would talk. But they weren't using words.

The next day, it happened again. My dad sat up in bed and began talking to someone directly in front of him. Only this time, he was relaxed and happy. He was nodding his head "yes" and agreeing with the person he was talking to. He laughed, and smiled, and his face glowed with love.

He could have been talking to my mother. Or his brother. It could have been his parents.

But it was an incredible thing to watch.

My dad was a role model to me my whole life. Even at the end of his life, he modeled strength, love, dignity, and the belief in another world.

I would love to do those two days over again.

And, finally, there's an afternoon I'd love to do over with Cliff. I met Cliff when he was working on his master's degree at Purdue. He rode a 10-speed bike, so I bought a bike so we could ride together. One day he took me to the local cemetery to teach me to ride it.

It was a hot, humid day, so Cliff decided to instruct me, not from riding along on his bike, but from sitting on the back end of his truck, in the shade, with his legs stretched out in front of him. He was the picture of comfort and hydration as he sucked a huge Slurpy from a straw.

The cemetery was not a good choice for my first lesson. Yes, it was peaceful – there was no one around. And there was a nice, circular path. But it was hilly. After I mastered getting on the bike and getting started, it began building up more speed than I was ready for.

Cliff saw that the bike was getting away from me (or he may have heard my cries for "help!"), and he called out: "Use your brakes."

But I sped past him so quickly, all I heard was: "Use your . . . "

"Use my WHAT?" I yelled the next time I sped past.

"Brakes. Use your brakes."

"Where are the brakes?" I cried, on my next time around. I'd never ridden a bike with hand brakes.

"On the handlebars!"

"Where?"

"Handlebars."

I squeezed the levers on the handlebars and went flying over the top of the bike.

That was lesson one.

He watched as I righted the bike and got back on.

Lesson two was changing gears.

"Switch gears." He called across to the far side of the cemetery.

"What are gears?"

"You need to be in a lower gear. Go to a lower gear."

"What's a lower gear?"

"A gear with a lower number than what you're on."

"Say what?"

I never did get the hang of gears.

But I will never forget the joy I had that afternoon. I felt as if I was flying as I rode around the path with Cliff cheering me on. And I'd love to do it again.

Wait.

I can still picture those four events.

I can still *feel* these four events.

So, I *can* do them again.

Any time I want.

Revenge of the Beauty Operators
(A Comedy in One Act)
by
Sara Jane Coffman

Characters:

CONNIE STEWART, an attractive, 22-year-old
hairstylist
TERRI ROBERTS, an assertive, 26-year-old hairstylist
CLIFF STOVER, a 30-year-old police officer
CHUCK McKENNA, Cliff's younger partner
TOM, a pizza deliveryman

TIME: *Friday evening*
SETTING: *The living room in Connie's house. There is a small dining room table with chairs, a desk with a telephone, two easy chairs, a window that has curtains with tie-backs, and a mirror on the wall. The front door is stage right. The kitchen is stage left.*

AT RISE: *Connie is pacing angrily. Terri is seated in an easy chair.*

CONNIE. Let me get this straight. He's been going to *your* place after work on Tuesdays and Thursdays?

TERRI. (*Nodding.*) Uh, huh.

CONNIE. For how long?

TERRI. About a month.

CONNIE. And he's been coming *here* on Mondays, Wednesdays, and Fridays! What a rat! I should have known something was up when he told me he was going to night school. Somehow that just didn't fit. I mean, he barely got through high school. How come all of a sudden he wants to take classes at *night*?

TERRI. How long have *you* been dating him?

CONNIE. Six months. (*Correcting herself.*) It would have been six months next week.

TERRI. (*Curious.*) Did you ever see him on weekends?

CONNIE. (*Sarcastic.*) Are you kidding? He lives for the weekend so he can go hunting with his dog. (Equally curious): Did you?

TERRI. No.

CONNIE. Do you know how much he paid to have that dog trained? $400.00! We used to go out to dinner, but then he had to save his money to send the dog to school. So he talked me into making him dinner. Oh, brother. I'm so dumb. (*Slumping into the other easy chair. Sighing.)* Where'd you meet him, anyway?

TERRI. At the Pizza Pen. He has this thing for pizza.

CONNIE. *(Dryly.)* Yes, I know.

TERRI. He didn't say he was dating anyone, so I invited him over. Don't feel bad. I've been cooking for him on Tuesdays and Thursdays. And he told me his class was on Mondays, Wednesdays, and Fridays.

CONNIE. So how'd you find out about me?

TERRI. I had this feeling something was up. I mean, I never saw him with any books. He never studied. So Wednesday night, I went to the police station. When he got off work, I followed him over here.

CONNIE. Then you saw him last night? And you didn't tell him?

TERRI. I almost did. Then I decided I'd rather come over and meet you.

CONNIE. *(Angry.)* I'm gonna rip his head off. How could he have done this to me? I thought we had an exclusive relationship.

TERRI. Well, I'm not that hung up on him. You can have him as far as I'm concerned.

CONNIE. (*Quietly.*) I'd sure like to hear his explanation.

TERRI. I think you ought to teach him a lesson.

CONNIE. (*Perking up.*) Yeah? (*Thinking.*) Listen would you mind sticking around? I could use your help.

TERRI. (*Grinning.*) I'd love to help!

CONNIE. (*Checking her watch.*) He's gonna be here any second. I think I'd like to talk to him alone before we let him know you're here. O.K.?

TERRI. Sure! Maybe I should go move my car.

CONNIE. Yeah. Put it in the garage. Then come back in through the kitchen and wait in the hallway.

TERRI. You know, it might be fun to tie him up.

CONNIE. We could use his handcuffs! (*Thinking.*) Listen, if I can get him standing up – right about here – and lay a big kiss on him – could you get his gun?

TERRI. Sure!

CONNIE. Then we can handcuff him. And then we can decide what we're gonna do.

TERRI. Great! See you in a minute. (*Exits stage right.*) (CONNIE *goes to the desk, pulls out a newspaper printout, and lays it on the table. A few seconds later, there's a knock at the door.* CONNIE *primps in the mirror, then opens the door.*)

CONNIE. (*Warmly.*) Hi! How's my big, touch cop? (*Gives him a big hug.*)

CHUCK. Your big, tough cop is tired. (*Noticing her.*) You look gorgeous! As usual. (*Comes in and makes himself at home.*)

CONNIE. It helps to work in a beauty salon.

CHUCK. Listen, what's for dinner? I missed lunch. We were out on calls all day, and I had a ton of paperwork right at shift change. (*Sits at dining room table.*)

CONNIE. Well, I've got good news and bad news. The bad news is that I haven't made dinner yet. (*Joining him at the table.*) I didn't have such a great day either. Mrs. Greene came in to have her hair colored – two hours early. Her appointment was at 11:00. She came in at 9:00. So I hurried and finished my first customer and squeezed her in. Then she complained about everything. The water was too cold, the shampoo had a funny smell, and, of course, then she didn't like the color – even though it's the same color I've always used. So she's coming back in tomorrow. Oh, and then, the clincher – Colleen's husband called, looking for her. She took the afternoon off to be with her boyfriend, so I had to lie to Frank and say she was out buying supplies.

CHUCK. You've had quite a day.

CONNIE. (*Dryly.*) You could say that.

CHUCK. Why don't we just order a pizza?

CONNIE. Great.

CHUCK. (*Going to the phone and dialing.*) The usual? (CONNIE *nods.*) Tom? Chuck McKenna. Listen, Connie doesn't feel like cooking tonight. (*He laughs.*) Yeah. The usual. Right. No. No breadsticks. (*Checking with* CONNIE *who nods "no."*) Great. (TO CONNIE.) Ten minutes.

CONNIE. Great!

CHUCK. (*Returning to table.*) Now, what's the good news?

CONNIE. (*Beaming.*) You're gonna be so proud of me!

CHUCK. Yeah? For what?

CONNIE. I've decided to go back to school!

CHUCK. (*Worried.*) You have?

CONNIE. Yeah! I mean, ever since you started taking classes, I've been thinking that I should, too. This schedule came in the mail – isn't this where you go? -- so I started looking through it. There're a bunch of classes I'd like to take.

CHUCK. Are you sure about this? I mean, night school's a lot of work.

CONNIE. I know. But if I take a class that meets on Tuesday and Thursday, we could go together!

CHUCK. (*Nervous.*) Together?

CONNIE. Wouldn't that be exciting?

CHUCK. (*Stands and paces.*) Connie, do you have any idea how distracting it would be for me to have you in the same class?

CONNIE. (*Going to him.*) Well, I wouldn't have to take the same class. I could take one in a room down the hall. What do you think, honey? (*Puts her arms around his neck and kisses him. He puts his arms around her and kisses back.* TERRI *enters from the hallway, gets his gun out of his holster, and points it at him.*)

TERRI. Hands up!

CHUCK. (*Confused.*) What???

TERRI. I said, put your hands up. (*He does.*)

CHUCK. What are *you* doing here?

TERRI. Get his handcuffs.

CHUCK. (*Backing up.*) Wait a minute . . .

TERRI. Don't move or I'll shoot. (*Waves the gun at him.*)

CHUCK. (*In a condescending tone.*) Terri put the gun down. You know you don't know how to use that.

TERRI. (*Off-handedly.*) You said I did pretty good when you took me to the shooting range.

CHUCK. (*Worried.*) Well, don't wave it around. It could go off. Somebody could get hurt. Please!

(CONNIE *gets his handcuffs from his belt.*)

CHUCK. Listen, what's the problem? Couldn't we talk about it? Terri, put the gun down. Please. . .

TERRI. (*Firmly.*) Sit down. (CONNIE *puts a chair in the center of the room.* CHUCK *sits.*) Put your hands behind your back.

CHUCK. O.K. O.K. I can see we have a little problem here, but it's nothing that can't be explained.

CONNIE. (*Putting his handcuffs on him.*) You can explain dating both of us at the same time? (CHUCK *is silent. To* TERRI): Put the gun in the desk. He's right. We don't want to *shoot* him.

TERRI. What if he doesn't stay in the chair?

CONNIE. (*Agreeing.*): Let's make sure he stays in the chair. (*She pulls the ties off the curtains and ties him to the chair.*) Now what?

TERRI. (*Putting the gun in the drawer.*) I think we ought to move his car. We don't know how long this is gonna take. Get his keys. (CONNIE *gets his keys from his pants pocket.*)

CHUCK. (*Alarmed.*) Wait a minute! Come on, you guys! You know I don't let anybody drive my Vette!

CONNIE. (*Calmly handing* TERRI *the keys.*) I'll move my car out of the garage and park it out front. You put the Vette in.

CHUCK. (*Hysterical.*) Terri doesn't know how to drive a stick!

CONNIE. That's why *she* gets to move it. (CHUCK *groans.*)

(TERRI *and* CONNIE *exit.* CHUCK *bounces his chair over to the telephone and gets the receiver off the hook. Hits "0" with his nose.*)

CHUCK. Operator! Get me the police. This is an emergency. (*Pause.*) Gary – Chuck. Listen, is Cliff still there? Get him for me, would you? (*Pause.*) Cliff – listen, I'm in trouble. I can't explain. I'm at 212 Oak Avenue. It's Connie's house. Get here fast. Hear me? FAST! (*He hangs up the receiver with his mouth and scoots the chair back. Girls enter from the kitchen.*)

CONNIE. (*To* TERRI.) So what kind of a guy would date two women at the same time?

TERRI. Let me think. Slimy. Insecure. Insensitive. Self-centered. Immature. (CHUCK *cringes at each adjective.*)

CONNIE. Can you think of *any* possible explanation?

TERRI. None.

CONNIE. O.K. So much for the explanation. Let's get down to the torture. Any ideas?

TERRI. (*Grinning.*) We could take his picture. Here's a big, macho cop getting tied up in his own handcuffs. How do you think the guys down at the station would react?

CONNIE. They'd love it! (CONNIE *gets her cell phone from desk.*)

CHUCK. Connie, don't take a picture! Please! Just tell me what you want.

CONNIE. We want to spend the evening humiliating you and making you miserable. Say "cheese." (CONNIE *takes a picture and shows it to* TERRI.) What do you think?

TERRI. Oh, I like his expression.

CHUCK. Terri!

TERRI. (*Mischievously.*) I have another idea. What do you think his buddies would say if he showed up in the locker room tomorrow with his legs shaved?

CHUCK. WHAT??

CONNIE. His legs shaved? I love it! How would he explain it?

TERRI. There's no way.

CONNIE. Pull his pant legs up. I'll get a razor. (TERRI *pulls his pants legs up while* CONNIE *exits to the kitchen.*)

CHUCK. (*Urgently trying to talk her out of this*): Terri, listen. Connie gets some crazy ideas sometimes. You don't really want to do this. Unlock the handcuffs and let me outta here. She'll calm down. Everybody'll feel better tomorrow. (CONNIE *reenters with a razor, shaving cream, bits of rope, hand towels, and perfume.*)

CONNIE. Look what I found! Some really stinky, old perfume! (*Let's* TERRI *smell it.*)

TERRI. That's awful!

CONNIE. And it lasts for days. Let's give him a good dose. (*She sprays perfume all over him.*)

CHUCK. Connie – don't! That stinks! Oh . . . great.

CONNIE. (*To* TERRI.) How's that?

TERRI. Great! Let's do his legs. (CHUCK *groans.*)

CONNIE. It might be easier if we tied them to the chair. Here. (*Hands* TERRI *a piece of rope. They each tie a leg.*) Hold still, Chuck.

CHUCK. Listen, you guys. Don't do this. I'll never hear the end of it.

CONNIE. That's O.K. with us. (*Puts shaving cream on his legs.*)

CHUCK. (*Complaining.*) That's cold!

TERRI. Shut up, Chuck. You're lucky we're using it. (*Doorbell rings. They all look up.*)

CONNIE. That must be the pizza. (*Goes to door while drying her hands on the towel.*)

CHUCK. Connie, don't let him in! (CONNIE *opens door.*)

TOM. (*Entering and crossing to table.*) One medium deluxe pizza. (*Stops when he sees* CHUCK.) Oh. Hey. How're you doing, Chuck?

CHUCK. (*Hiding his embarrassment.*) Fine, Tom.

TOM. (*Looking at handcuffs.*) You O.K.?

CHUCK. Oh, yeah. Sure. (TOM *doesn't buy that.*) We're just playing a little game. Right?

TERRI. Right!

CONNIE. Right!

TOM. (*Sniffing.*) What's that smell?

CHUCK. Oh. Uh. Connie dropped a bottle of perfume.

TOM. She drop it on you? (*Everybody laughs.*) Well, as long as everybody's all right.

CHUCK. We're fine, Tom. What do we owe you?

TOM. (*Putting pizza on table.*) $9.50

CONNIE. Here, Chuck. Let me help you get your wallet. (*She reaches into his pocket, pulls out his wallet, and hands* TOM *a bill.*) Here's a $20, Tom. Keep the change.

TOM. A $10.00 tip? Gee, thanks, Chuck!

CHUCK. (*Dryly.*) My pleasure.

TOM. Well, if you need anything else, just holler.

TERRI. Did you get breadsticks?

CONNIE. No.

TERRI. I'd love some breadsticks.

CONNIE. O.K. How about an order of breadsticks?
    And some cokes.

TOM. Breadsticks and cokes. Back in a jiffy. (*He exits
    with a big smile.*) TERRI *and* CONNIE *sit at table
    and start to eat. They ignore* CHUCK.)

TERRI. So, how long have you worked at the Hairport?

CONNIE. Three years. It's a decent place to work if
    you can get along with the boss.

TERRI. Tell me about it. I used to work there.

CONNIE. (*Surprised.*) You did?

TERRI. Yeah. Is Michelle still up to her old tricks? (CHUCK *clears his throat.*)

CONNIE. Oh, yeah.

TERRI. And does Mrs. Greene still complain about her hair color?

CONNIE. She was in today! (CHUCK *clears his throat, louder.* CONNIE *turns to* CHUCK.) Yes?

CHUCK. (*Humbly.*) Could I have a piece? I missed lunch today, remember?

CONNIE. (*Waving a piece under his nose.*) You want some pizza? Forget it.

TERRI. (*Diabolically.*) Hey, you know what would be even better than a razor?

CONNIE. What?

TERRI. One of those electric jobbies that pulls the hair out by the roots.

CONNIE. (*Shivers.*) My sister gave me one one time, but I've been too chicken to use it.

TERRI. Oh, they're evil. They have a steel cord that vibrates at a real high speed. It grabs hold of the hair and sucks it out – roots and all.

CONNIE. It sounds like the kind of present my sister would give me. Come on, it's in the basement. We're gonna have to move some boxes.

(*They exit, eating pizza. CHUCK groans. Then he eyes the pizza, scoots his chair toward the table, and tries to get a piece with his mouth. There's a knock on the door.*)

CHUCK. (*Loud whisper.*) Come in. (*Another knock. Louder whisper.*) Come in. (CLIFF *enters.*)

CLIFF. (*Entering and surveying the room.*) What the hell happened to you?

CHUCK. (*Urgently.*) Don't ask. Just get me out of these damned things. Quick. Before they come back!

CLIFF. (*Laughing.*) Are those your cuffs?

CHUCK. This isn't funny. Get me outta here.

CLIFF. (*Sniffing.*) What's that smell? Is that you?

CHUCK. They sprayed me with perfume.

CLIFF. (*Sitting in a chair backwards.*) You seem to be in a blind, Romeo. How're you planning to get out of this?

CHUCK. I was planning on having you get me out of this. Use your key.

CLIFF. (*Chuckling.*): This is great! What happened?

CHUCK. (*Abashed.*) Connie found out I've been out with Terri.

CLIFF. Connie did this?

CHUCK. They both did. They're in the basement looking for things to torture me with. They're gonna be back any minute. Come on, Cliff!

CLIFF. (*Noticing* CHUCK's *empty holster*) Where's your gun?

CHUCK. (*Embarrassed.*) They took it.

CLIFF. You let two women take your gun? (*Amused.*) Wish I could've seen that. (*Teasing*). Do we need a little more basic training for this job, or do we just need to be a little more careful about who we date?

CHUCK. Cliff!!

CLIFF. What's the shaving cream for?

CHUCK. They're gonna shave my legs.

CLIFF. (*Laughing.*) How're you going to explain that down at the station?

CHUCK. I won't have to if you just hurry. I'm telling you – they're mad! They're gonna be even madder when they find you here.

CLIFF. From the looks of things, I think maybe I should leave and let them have you. You know, I told you this was gonna happen. You just don't mess around with two women at the same time. (TERRI *and* CONNIE *return and stop when they see* CLIFF. CLIFF *stands up and speaks in an official tone.*) There seems to be a problem here, ladies. Can I help?

(*Pause. Nobody moves.* CLIFF *takes charge.*)

CLIFF. Why don't you let me take this prisoner off your hands? (*Another pause. Then* TERRI, *regaining her composure, walks deliberately up to* CLIFF.)

TERRI. You must be Cliff, Chuck's partner. He's told me a lot about you. Especially that you're a great kisser! (*She puts her arms around his neck and lays*

a big kiss on him. Surprised, he kisses back.
CONNIE *quickly moves in and gets his gun.*)

CONNIE. Hands up! (*He puts his hands up.*)

CHUCK. Way to go, Cliff.

CLIFF. (*Pointedly.*) What are you doing?

TERRI. Sorry. We can't let you go. We're not through with him yet.

CLIFF. (*Sternly.*) Are you serious?

CONNIE. We're not gonna hurt him. We just want to teach him a lesson.

CLIFF. It's not a *permanent* thing? You're just gonna embarrass him and send him back to the troops?

CONNIE. Right.

CLIFF. O.K. Put the gun down so I know nobody's gonna get hurt. (*Amused.*) I'd kind of like to stay and watch anyway.

CONNIE. Get his handcuffs. (TERRI *does.*) O.K. Sit down. (*He sits in a chair next to* CHUCK. TERRI *handcuffs* CLIFF. CONNIE *puts the gun in the drawer with the other one.*)

CHUCK. (*To* CLIFF.) I hope you didn't have any plans for tonight.

CLIFF. As a matter of fact, I didn't. Do you want to introduce me to your friends?

CHUCK. (*Unhappily.*) Terri Robert, Connie Stewart – Cliff Stover.

TERRI. Hi!

CONNIE. Hi!

CLIFF. Hi! (*To* TERRI): You know you look familiar. Didn't you lock your keys in your car at the mall a couple of weeks ago?

TERRI. (*Sitting.*) And you got the door open for me! I can't believe I did that! I never lock my keys in the car. That was so stupid!

CLIFF. Hey, a lot of people do that. I was glad to help.

CHUCK. If you want to hear something stupid, ask Cliff about the time he shot himself in the arm.

CLIFF. (*Embarrassed.*) Yeah.

CONNIE. (*Sitting in easy chair.*) Chuck told me about that. You were trying to arrest somebody.

CLIFF. Two somebodies. One was behind me holding my arms behind my back, and the other one was in front of me trying to mess up my face.

TERRI. What happened?

CLIFF. Well, I managed to get my arm loose and I went for my gun and as I was shooting, the guy behind me let my left arm go, and it ended up getting in the way.

TERRI. (*Impressed.*) Did you shoot him?

CLIFF. Yeah. I got him in the leg.

TERRI. But the bullet went through your arm? I'll bet that hurt!

CLIFF. Yeah, a bit.

TERRI. (*Concerned.*) Gee are the handcuffs too tight?

CHUCK. Nobody's asked me about my handcuffs.

CLIFF. No, they're fine. I'll let you know if they start to hurt.

CHUCK. Nobody's asked me about my handcuffs!

(*There's a knock on the door.*)

CHUCK. Oh, great.

CONNIE. That must be Tom. (*She goes to door and opens it.*) Hi, Tom!

TOM. Hi, Connie! (*He enters the room and stops when he sees Cliff.*) Well, I'll be. Hi, Cliff!

CLIFF. Hi, Tom! How's it going?

TOM. Not bad. (*The men all eye each other.* CONNIE *takes the food from him.*)

CONNIE. How much do we owe you?

TOM. Oh, it's on the house.

CONNIE. Thanks, Tom! (*Opens door for him to leave.* TOM *slowly backs out.*)

TOM. Well, if you need anything else . . . . You guys sure you're O.K.?

CHUCK. We're fine, Tom.

CLIFF. We're fine, Tom. Appreciate your concern.
(TOM *exits.* TERRI *and* CONNIE *sit at the table, drinking, eating, and ignoring the men.*)

TERRI: So, what do we have here?

CONNIE. Well, let's see. It looks like we've got two police officers tied up.

TERRI. Is anybody gonna be looking for them?

CONNIE. I doubt it.

TERRI. Good.

CONNIE. (*Smiling.*) We also have Chuck's wallet and the keys to his car. (*Holds them up.*)

TERRI. So why don't we go trash his car?

CHUCK. (*Screaming.*) NO!!

CONNIE. I think we've hit a cord, here. You don't suppose he thinks more of that Corvette than he does of us? Let's go. (*Starts to exit.*)

CLIFF. Hold on, ladies. Let's think about this for a minute. You don't wanna do anything illegal. Right now you're not in any trouble. But if you start damaging property, that's a different story. Besides, you gals are a lot more clever than that.

TERRI. We are?

CLIFF. Sure. Listen, I understand where you're coming from. You have every right to be upset.

CHUCK. Whose side are you on?

CLIFF. Not yours. I think we owe these women an apology. (*To women.*) Now, if I were you, instead of trashing his car, I'd take his credit cards and go buy something expensive. That would make *me* feel better.

TERRI. Me, too!

CHUCK. CLIFF!!

CONNIE. I know what I want. A fake fur coat. Let's see what he's got. (*Looks through CHUCK's wallet and pulls out two credit cards.*) Here we go. One for you and one for me.

CHUCK. CONNIE!!

CONNIE. (*To TERRI.*) I'm gonna go change my clothes. Then you and I are going to do the mall. (*Exits stage left.*)

TERRI. (*To* CLIFF.) Did anybody ever tell you you've got a great head of hair?

CLIFF. I do?

TERRI. Where do you get it cut?

CLIFF. That barber shop at the Service Center.

TERRI. You outta come in and have it *styled*.

CLIFF. (*Embarrassed.*) I don't know about a beauty shop.

TERRI. We have lots of male customers. I'll bet you've never had a manicure, either.

CLIFF. Well, no.

TERRI. You should tell your wife that's what you want for your next birthday.

CLIFF. I don't think she'd be too interested. She divorced me three years ago.

TERRI. (*Interested.*) Oh?

CHUCK. Yeah. Cliff came home from work one day and found a note. His wife said her cats were unhappy, so she packed them up and left.

TERRI. No kidding.

CLIFF. I still have the note.

TERRI. Well, if you're interested, here's my card. (*Puts her business card in his shirt pocket.*)

CLIFF. You know . . . if Chuck wouldn't mind, I'd kinda like to take you to a movie some time.

TERRI. O.K.

CLIFF. What kind of movies do you like?

TERRI. Actually, I'm sort of a romantic. But Chuck only likes Rambo movies.

CLIFF. I love romantic movies. What are you doing tonight?

TERRI. Well I *was* going shopping.

CLIFF. Why don't I take you?

TERRI. O.K.

CLIFF. I could drive better with these off. (TERRI *unlocks his handcuffs.*) Hey, Chuck, you guys wanna go with us? (CONNIE *enters.*)

CHUCK. I don't know. (*To* CONNIE.) Connie – Cliff and Terri are going to the mall. You wanna go?

CONNIE. (*Pointedly.*) We have some unfinished business, Chuck.

CLIFF. We'll wait in the car. (CLIFF *gets his gun and he and* TERRI *exit.*)

CONNIE. I can't believe . . .

CHUCK. You wouldn't believe . . .

CONNIE. You first.

CHUCK. (*Passionately.*) You wouldn't believe how glad I am this is out on the open. I've been feeling rotten. Ask Cliff.

CONNIE. (*Upset.*) How could you lie to me like that? I thought we had an exclusive relationship?

CHUCK. I don't know. It just happened. For awhile it was great, thinking two really neat women could both like me. But then . . . (*Shakes his head.*) But I'm not serious about Terri. She knows that.

CONNIE. But you lied to me about going to night school. You know I can't stand people who lie. I think all the liars in the world should have to go off and live together on a desert island so they can all sit around and just lie to each other. (*Beat.*) Chuck, I want to have a relationship with you, but it's got to be an honest relationship. I won't settle for anything less.

CHUCK. Lying to you was awful for me, too. Connie, I don't want to lose you. I learned my lesson. I won't do it again. (*Beat.*) Believe me, I couldn't do it again. (*Weak smile.*) A fake fur coat, huh?

CONNIE. Uh, huh.

CHUCK. We can do that.

CONNIE. (*Firmly.*) And I'm serious about going to night school.

CHUCK. You can do that.

CONNIE. I mean, I want both of us to go.

CHUCK. You really want me to go to school?

CONNIE. Yes.

CHUCK. Oh. Well, bring that list of classes. We can look at it after we buy the coat. Now, will you untie me?

(CONNIE *unties him and unlocks the handcuffs. He dries the shaving cream off, rolls down his pants legs, and gets his gun.*)

CHUCK. You really had me going there. You wouldn't really have used this thing on me, would you? (*Handling electric razor.*)

CONNIE. Probably not. But if you ever lie to me again . . .

CHUCK. I hear you. (*Pause.*) And I love you. (*He kisses her.*)

CONNIE. Well, at least we'll have the mall to ourselves tonight.

CHUCK. What do you mean?

CONNIE. With the way you smell – anywhere we go tonight, we'll have the place to ourselves!

(*They exit laughing. A moment later,* CHUCK *returns, grabs a piece of pizza and exits, eating the pizza.*)

197

THE END

PRODUCTION NOTES

CHARACTERS: *2 female, 3 male*

COSTUMES: *2 police uniforms, one pizza deliveryman uniform*

PROPS: *purse with set of car keys, single set of car keys, 2 pairs of handcuffs (and keys) and two fake guns. Newspaper printout of college courses. Cell phone. Disposable razor, electric razor, shaving cream, 2 tie-backs from curtains, 2 hand towels, bottle of perfume. Wallet with a bill in it. A business card.*

Made in the USA
Columbia, SC
05 March 2019